Whatever Became Of Grace?

*Stories of Hope for Preaching and Teaching
in a Graceless World*

John Pennington

CSS Publishing Company, Inc.

Lima, Ohio

WHATEVER BECAME OF GRACE?

FIRST EDITION

Copyright © 2020

by CSS Publishing Co., Inc.

Library of Congress Cataloging-in-Publication Data

Names: Pennington, John, 1945- author. Title: Whatever became of grace? : stories of hope in a graceless world / John Pennington. Description: First edition. | Lima, Ohio : CSS Publishing Company, Inc., 2020. Identifiers: LCCN 2020036940 | ISBN 9780788030055 | ISBN 9780788030062 (ebook) Subjects: LCSH: Grace (Theology) Classification: LCC BT761.3 .P46 2020 | DDC 234--dc23 LC record available at https://lccn.loc.gov/2020036940

For more information about CSS Publishing Company resources, visit our website at www.csspub.com, email us at csr@csspub.com, or call (800) 241-4056.

e-book:
ISBN-13: 978-0-7880-3006-2
ISBN-10: 0-7880-3006-X

ISBN-13: 978-0-7880-3005-5
ISBN-10: 0-7880-3005-1

DIGITALLY PRINTED

To Sandra and John,
whose steadfast grace inspires my hope

Table Of Contents

Introduction

In the early 1970's, a psychiatrist by the name of Karl Menninger wrote a book titled, *Whatever Became of Sin* that became extremely popular, especially among preachers. I remember thinking at the time, "Whatever became of sin? It's doing quite well for itself the last time I checked." A better question would be whatever became of grace.

The Christian church has had no problem finding sin. It's been doing that for generations. Indeed, there are many of "God's detectives" scouring the countryside, performing the task of "sin-hunting" like their forefathers, the Puritans.

Frederic Greeves reminded us in his book, *The Meaning of Sin* that Jesus used the noun "sin" on only six occasions and the verb "sin" on only three occasions, but by the time the church was started, Paul used those words 91 times! At its very outset, the church was obsessed with sin.[1]

It is always the temptation of "the righteous" to find sins that they haven't committed, so they might feel superior to those who have. As my dear friend, the late John Claypool used to say, "We judge most harshly those who sin differently from us."[2] For some reason, it is an ugly part of our human nature that we must find "outsiders" to assure us that we are "insiders," and if outsiders can't readily be found, we will make some as quickly as possible.

So, the church has set out to "weigh sins" — this sin is worse than that sin. We not only know how to find sins we haven't committed, but we know how to weigh which of the commandments are more important than the other commandments, and which is the most fatal. A serious problem for the church in this endeavor is that God never furnished us with the proper scales for such a task. It appears only God can accurately weigh sins, and God's scales consist of a mercy that

1 Frederic Greeves, T*he Meaning of Sin* (London; Epworth Press 2017), 102
2 John Claypool, "Easter and the Fear of Death", 1997.

outweighs the heaviest of sins.

One can attend many, if not most, churches today and find little grace there whatsoever. In fact, many sermons that are preached in Christian churches are sermons about us, not God, and "us" is not good news.

The season of Lent appears to be the worst of the worst for the church. For many, it's a time to take an official time-out from the gospel so that we might feel guilty again. What the church hasn't figured out, apparently, is that people feel quite terrible about themselves already, without any help from the church. None is necessary. What *is* necessary is the antidote.

To use the season of Lent to make people feel guilty is a gross misuse of the season. One young lady I know, who felt particularly guilty about her sins, went to her pastor during Lent to tell him she was feeling heavy guilt brought on by the way Lent was being observed in her church. His advice was, "Don't come to church during Lent." *What?* Here's a word to that pastor. Preach the gospel during Lent, as in any other season of the church year, and never tell people that if they can't endure your guilt sessions to not attend church!

In his letter to the Romans, Paul was quite specific about this. He said, "*The law is good, but sin dwells within me. I can will what is right, but I cannot do it. I find when I want to do good, evil lies close at hand. If it had not been for the law, I would not have known sin. Because when I read, "you shall not covet," I started coveting! Wretched man that I am! Who will rescue me from this body of death?*" This was written by one of the greatest Christians who ever lived! And then, he answered his own question, "*Who will deliver me? Thanks be to God through Jesus Christ our Lord.*"

Paul learned instead of saying, "wretched person that I am," to say, "how good God is to forgive me." *That* is the message of the church. It's a message about the goodness of God, not the badness of us. A long time ago, God had to decide, "What am I going to do with these humans? I gave them the law to tell them how to live, and they can't keep the law!" At that moment, God had a decision to make. Would God be punitive and angry, or would God be merciful to our human failures? God chose to be merciful, and every service at every church should proclaim this good news.

Simply sharing the rules does not work. Paul said it didn't work for him. Israel never kept the commandments, and they were the ones to whom the commandments were given. If the law had been good enough, there would have been no need for the coming of Christ. Jesus was God's answer to what God would do about his errant children.

So, whatever became of grace? Where or when did the church lose its mission of preaching the good news? Where or when did we revert to the rule book and sin-hunting?

In the pages that follow, I want to make the case for grace. I want to speak of a good and merciful God, and I want to point out what I believe the church should be doing every time it opens its doors, and that is, answering Paul's question, "Who will rescue me from this body of death?"

Chapter One

How God Feels About You

When Jesus was baptized, no sooner had he come up out of the water than the heavens were torn apart, the Spirit descended like a dove, and a voice from heaven said, "*You are my son (child), the beloved, with whom I am well pleased.*" The most remarkable thing about this statement is the fact that it came up front, before Jesus had done anything to earn it. It happened before he preached his first sermon, before he healed his first illness, before he comforted his first bereaved person, and before he forgave his first sinner. It was pure gift. "You are mine, and you are loved."

That's what it means to be "beloved." Again and again, that's how the Bible refers to you and me: "The beloved," those with unearned love. All of us want it. All of us need it. We're like the little girl listening to her daddy in the car one day. "You're just a delight to me, honey. You're a wonderful daughter. You're a good sister to your brother. You help your mother. You make us all very happy." And she looked up at him and said, "More, daddy! More!"

We're like the little boy who played baseball on his high school team. His dad said to him over and over, "Someday, son, you're going to play in the big leagues." He was saying that one day after his son came home from a big game, and the boy said, "Did you come to the game today? Did you see what I did out there? I struck out four times!" And his dad said, "Yes, but what a swing!"

The boy played catcher on the team, so he said, "Did you see me try to throw out the runner at second base? I threw it ten feet over the second baseman's head!" And his dad said, "Yes, but what an arm!" God blesses all of us like that. It's just hard for some of us to hear it because we are so obsessed with our failures. We know who we are. We know what we've done. We know we're not who we promised God we would be. We've failed, all of us, and so we think we don't deserve to be called "the beloved." And we don't. Thankfully, deserve has nothing to do with it, because it's a free gift from God.

God looks at each of us and says, "It's not because of you that I bless you. It's because of me. I choose to look at all my children and say, 'I'm in your corner. You're the apple of my eye. I love you. Let's go make the future better than the past. Trust me to do that for you.'"

That is the deepest meaning of the cross. It is a word to people who have sinned. That's what God did for Israel. He didn't give up on Israel, and they failed him again and again. He didn't give up on his disciples even though they failed him again and again. Why would God not do that for you?

Some people don't believe this because they've never experienced unconditional love before. Who else loves you without conditions? Maybe your dog or your cat if you're lucky, so it's hard to believe that we can't do anything to make God love us more than God already loves us, and we can't do anything to make God stop loving us. To trust that is what it is to be a Christian, to simply trust that there is more mercy in God than there is sin in you, and to know there is no sin so great that not even God can forgive it.

Others have trouble believing because it is so big. Fred Craddock used to tell of the little boy who wanted to go to the circus, but he couldn't afford a ticket. The man selling tickets saw him standing there and said, "Son, if you will come tomorrow for the matinee, I'll let you in free!"

The little boy could hardly sleep that night and could hardly pay attention at school. As soon as school was over, he ran straight down to the circus. There was this big group of children standing there, and the man said, "All right, all you children get to go in free today. Go right on in." The little boy just stood there. He said, "You mean *everybody* gets in free? You mean I'm not the only one? *All* of us get in free?" "That's right, son, all of you." The little boy, disappointed, turned and walked away.[3]

Why did he do that? He had to have outsiders to assure him of being an insider. Some people can't accept the gospel because they don't want God to just love everybody, even the ones they deem to be sinners and outsiders.

Burnham Ledford told of one day going to see his great, great grandmother. She was very old and blind, and he was afraid of her. He'd never met her before, and now he had to go meet her. He didn't know what to expect. When they arrived at her house his parents said, "We have brought Burnham to see you, grandmother."

She said, "Bring him here." Burnham said they had to push him, because he was so afraid. But then he said, "When I got over to her, her hands were gentle, as she carefully touched my cheek and eyes and mouth. And then she said something I'll never forget. She said, 'This boy is one of ours. This boy is in our family all right. This one belongs to us.'"[4]

Even so, the gentle hands of God are touching you right now. And God is saying, "This one belongs to me." To trust that is what it means to be a Christian. It has nothing to do with how good or how bad you are. It has everything to do with how good God is.

Roberta Bondi, who taught at Candler School of Theology in Atlanta, said that back in the 1960's she thought of herself as an atheist because she was just sure God hated her for her sins. She says she got that idea from the church of her childhood and from the Christians she knew. But one day, while she was reading an assignment in graduate school, she came across an ancient text, written by a sixth-century bishop named Philoxenus, that was addressed to his fellow monks in the monastery. It read: "We monks ought not to judge one another, because God judges us much more leniently than we human beings are equipped to do."

Roberta said those words bowled her over. They spoke convincingly to her heart of a God she had not been able to imagine, a God whose

3   From Craddock cassette tape, Biblical Bases for Evangelism, Christian Council of Metro Atlanta
4   Aiken Standard, printed sermon by Dr. Fred Andrea

kindness and love far outweighed any interest in her inadequacies. She wrote, "Those words conveyed to me that I ought not to be intimidated by religious people who are judgmental, because their judgmentalism has very little God in it. It is from reading those words from a sixth-century bishop that I first came to identify myself as a Christian."[5]

She had identified the voice of Jesus in that ancient monk, and it was all she needed to get her to trust God's great love for her. Jesus said, "My sheep hear my voice." It was a very distinctive voice. It isn't difficult to distinguish it from other voices. Anyone who came to him never felt put down or scolded. They always felt loved, no matter what mistake they had made or what sin they had committed. It was a loving voice, and it was a comforting voice. Jesus was never combative, divisive, or accusatory. He never demanded anyone's punishment, never wanted to get even with anyone, and never excluded anyone from his love.

Jesus believed we would know his voice from all the others. To share that voice in the preaching of the gospel is the calling of today's preachers. It's never about us. It's always about God. You take that voice into everything you read and everything you hear, and you'll know right away if you are hearing the gospel. You even take that voice into your reading of the Bible, and it will help you to interpret the Bible. That's what it means to have a theology. Some biblical texts will carry the gospel, and others will need to have the gospel carried to them, but you will know the difference if you listen for his voice.

One group of Christians made this observation as to how to know the voice of Jesus. In the early part of the nineteenth century the Disciples of Christ laid out guidelines for Bible study, and one of them was this: "If you would understand the scripture and recognize the voice of Christ in your life, you must live within understanding distance of God." In other words, the way sheep know the difference between the shepherd and a stranger is they have lived with the shepherd long enough to know the voice. There simply is no substitute for that.

It is truly good news to know that you are loved, and it isn't something

5   The Christian Century, Nov. 2, 2004

that you earn. I read once of a young woman who had become addicted to alcohol. Her life was turning into a living hell, but by the grace of God she had gotten into that wonderful fellowship of redemption called Alcoholics Anonymous. They taught her that she could be different, and one night at a meeting she heard a wise old man stand up and say, "Every saint has a past, and every sinner has a future."

She said that insight was electrifying to her. Every saint has a past. If you look deeply into anybody you consider to be godly and saintly, they will be the first person to tell you there's a lot back there they are ashamed of, but they have made an important discovery: Because of the great mercy of God, every sinner has a future. And God has helped them make the future different from the past.

Hear it once again. You are "the beloved." You didn't do anything to earn it, so you can't forfeit it. Your assignment is only to trust it and watch it change you.

This often involves forgiving yourself. It is a very arrogant thing to believe you can sin so badly that not even God can forgive it. When Jesus prayed from the cross, "Father, forgive them," that prayer surely included you. No one is too broken to mend. Trusting that God loves you means trusting God can forgive you.

Often, as with Roberta Bondi, we may have been led to believe that God doesn't forgive us because other people won't forgive us. My teacher, John Carlton, used to say that moral indignation about others doesn't have an ounce of God in it and is never distinctively Christian. Only when we can say, "There but for the grace of God go I," does it reveal the spirit of God in our lives. Never equate the lack of forgiveness in others with the forgiveness of God.

All of us could have lived our lives better. We're all carrying a sack of rocks. Failure is our human condition. No one has done it perfectly. The God who raised Jesus from the dead can raise you from whatever sin has you buried in shame. God's forgiveness gives you full permission to forgive yourself. Begin that forgiveness this way: Instead of saying, "What a miserable sinner I am," say instead, "How good God is to forgive me!" That's the beginning of self forgiveness.

Jesus spent his entire life teaching us that God looks at each one of us and says, "I'm in your corner. You have my favor. You don't earn it, because it's on the house. I still believe in you, even after you mess up. Nothing can separate you from my love, not even your sin. I can repair you, because I take delight in you. My favor rests on you." That's why they call it "good news."

Even some of the ancient Jewish rabbis knew that. They used to tell the story of the Red Sea this way:

"God was busy, so he turned the job of parting the Red Sea over to a committee of angels, and they said, 'We'll take care of it.' When the Israelites came to the water, the angels parted the water, and they went across. But when the Egyptians came to the water, the angels turned the water loose, and chariots, horses, and soldiers were all tumbling and drowning. And the angels were dancing and saying, 'We got 'em! We got 'em!'"

"When God heard the commotion and looked down to see what was happening, he turned to the angels and said, 'You'll never do anything important for me again.' And they said, 'Why? We got 'em!' And God said, 'The Egyptians are my children too.'"

Now, why did the rabbis tell the story that way? It was because they knew God's nature. Even before Jesus came to show us, they knew God to be a loving and forgiving God. That's the church's message today. It's not half the message. It's not one of the messages. It *is the* message. That's the message every heart yearns to hear. You are loved.

What a wonderful gospel we have. Bishop Kenneth Goodson told how he once met Dr. Christian Barnard, the first surgeon to perform a heart transplant. The bishop asked the doctor, "What's it like to do a heart transplant?" Barnard said, "It's an awesome thing to reach your hand into someone's chest and hold their heart in your hand." But you know what? Preachers do that every Sunday, when they preach the gospel, instead of moralistic "musts, oughts, and shoulds."

Tom Long, a former renowned professor at Emory's Candler

Seminary, said that when he was just a teenager, his uncle Ed ran a service station in a small South Carolina town. Ed was a wonderful man. People loved him. But when he was still a young man, his big heart failed him, and he died. The family gathered to make arrangements. Their pastor was out of town on vacation, and Tom's family insisted that the pastor not interrupt his vacation. But he said he wanted to come back, so he drove half the night and all the next morning.

When he arrived back home, he went by the house to see the family. Tom said he would never forget the arrival of the preacher. The family was all together in the living room, and somebody looked out the window and said, "The preacher's here."

Long said what the preacher did not know and could not know was that the atmosphere in that living room changed the moment he stepped out of the car. He had brought with him more than he would ever know. He had brought the personified grace of God.[6] That is something the church can do every Sunday, if it only will. It is the most important thing any church and any preacher can ever do.

One example happened at a hospital where a young man was dying, fully aware and frightened, so the nurses called for the chaplain. The chaplain came and leaned over and held the boy's hand and whispered something over and over in his ear until he relaxed, and in a few minutes, he died.

The nurses said, "That was amazing. What did you say to calm him down like that? We need to know." The chaplain said, "I just repeated over and over again, 'I love you and God loves you. I forgive you and God forgives you.'"[7] That is grace. Not just for the dying, but for the living. That is the gospel that needs to be shared every week by the church.

There is a moving story of a Christian from a church somewhere, who regularly visited patients in a nursing home every week. He always held their hands, and on one occasion when he went to visit a patient,

6   Sermon delivered by Dr. Tom Long
7   Sermon delivered by Dr. Tom Long

he wasn't in his room. The visitor asked where the patient was, and was told that he was very sick, near death, and had been moved to a private room. They said, "He's unconscious, but you can visit if you like. His children are all there."

The visitor went in and told them who he was; he held the man's hand and said a short prayer. When he said *amen*, the old man squeezed his hand. And his daughter said, "You know, he's been waiting for you. He told us he couldn't die till Jesus came and held his hand. We told him that, after he leaves this world, Jesus will hold his hand. But he said, 'No, once a week Jesus comes and holds my hand, and I don't want to leave until I have a chance to hold it just once more.'"

The visitor said, "Oh my, he thought I was Jesus, did he?" And the daughter said, "He couldn't tell the difference." In our churches across the land, when preachers stand to preach, people need to hear what Jesus would tell them. They need to know they are loved. They need to know they are forgiven. They need to hear the preacher's voice as the voice of Jesus.[8] Is it so hard to understand... that our one message is the voice of grace? It's the one thing that is the church's specialty. People can get moralism other places. They can get guilt all by themselves. But grace... that is the church's unique calling.

---

8   Sermon delivered by Dr. Tom Long

Chapter Two

What God Expects From The Church

I can still remember a practice that was done when I was in elementary school that has to be one of the worst things ever taught. I'm speaking of something that the teachers taught us to do that was clearly wrong. Some of my classmates actually became good at it.

In fact, some of them enjoyed it so much that, when the teacher left the room for one reason or another, they would wave their hands and asked to be chosen for the task. It was a practice called, "taking names." Remember that?

The teacher would say, "I'm leaving the room for a few minutes, but I want you to remain very quiet, so I'm asking Mary, Bob, Susan, Jimmy, whomever… to take names." It was the most dreaded of all threats. They will take your name!

Well, I didn't want anybody to take my name. My mother and daddy gave it to me, and I didn't want anybody taking it! But when the teacher left the room, the name takers would glare over the room with a self-righteous smirk on their faces, just looking for someone to utter a sound. And it never failed, someone would pinch my leg or hit my arm, and startled I would say, "Oh!" And they'd take my name.

I would protest and say, "I was just startled because someone hit me. I was not talking." And they would say, "But you are now." And they'd write down my name again. I thought that was a terrible thing for the teachers to teach. "Today class, we're going to have a lesson on how to become a rat fink, that snitches." I thought so then and I know so now. Nobody should ever take another person's name.

But it happens all the time in churches. The name God has given us is beloved, but anytime someone can get us to compromise our grace, that is, our compassion, kindness, and forgiveness, they have taken our name! One very prominent scholar has said, "I had to quit going to church, because I couldn't find any grace there." Could that be the reason so many others have given up on the church?

My friend and mentor, the late John Carlton, used to describe worship as a thirsty land crying out for rain, a candle in the act of being kindled, a drop in quest of the ocean, and a voice in the night calling for help. It is grace and grace alone that fills such needs.

I took copious notes in John's class on worship. Among the most memorable are these words: "I personally feel that good preaching ought to inspire and enable people. My observation is that most people today are carrying about all of the load they can stand to carry. They don't need a preacher to stand over them with a moral whip, goading them on. No one attending a worship service should leave at the point of moral despair. Jesus did not come into the world to tell us how bad we are, but how wonderful life can be and how great God is."

"How sad," John said, "that anyone should ask, 'What did he preach about,' and I received the answer, 'I don't know; he never said. He shot a sermon in the air; it fell to earth I know not where. The sermon was entirely too long. It needed to be cut in half, either half would have been appropriate.'"

I remember hearing a great songwriter once say, "Songs can be healing or they can be damaging. The responsibility of a good songwriter is to always leave hope in his or her songs." The same thing can be said of sermons.

I remember concluding a worship service in my first church, my "camel hair and leather girdle days," when a woman attempting to compliment me said, "I don't feel like I've been to church unless my toes have been stepped on." God bless her. She was in dire need of a good psychiatrist, not a preacher, and as I saw myself as an Old Testament prophet, it would have been a good idea if I had accompanied her. Our message is hope and grace.

Another one of my teachers, Ted Adams, once told of a New England town that experienced a blackout one night. Everything was plunged into complete darkness because of a power failure, and the only thing showing was the illuminated cross on the steeple of a church in the middle of town, because it had its own generator.

Dr. Adams used to point to that and say, "The church runs on a different power system than the world. Our power system is the love and grace of God. When everything is dark, that's when those of us who bear the name "Christian" shine the best." He was assuming, of course, that we would not forget our unique purpose.

We were born by the grace of God. We didn't earn it. We've been redeemed by the grace of God. We didn't earn that either. We've been given the church, and we didn't earn that gift. But when the church loses its grace, it has lost its entire power system.

Jesus told his disciples, including today's church, "I'm going to give you a gift, so you might continue what I'm trying to do. I'm going to give you the keys of the kingdom." Of course, keys are used to lock and to unlock things, and the grace of God in Jesus Christ unlocked people from their past and set them free on a new future. The only thing Jesus ever used the keys to lock was evil, things like blindness, seizures, illness, and guilt. He bound all of that, but he used the keys to set people free. Now those keys belong to the church.

In 1962, Fred Rogers, of PBS fame, entered Pittsburgh Theological Seminary. He could only take a few courses at a time, and one of the courses he took was a course in theology taught by Dr. Bill Orr. One day the class was discussing Martin Luther, and Fred asked him about the hymn Luther wrote titled "A Mighty Fortress." The hymn says one little word shall fell the prince of darkness.

And Fred asked, "What do you think that one little word was that Luther was talking about?" Dr. Orr said, "I think that word is forgiveness, Fred. There's one thing evil cannot stand, and that is forgiveness. Evil will battle against it in every life, in every group, in every family, and in every church. It's the one thing that conquers evil, and it's the one thing God used to conquer evil."[9] The grace of God is the tool God has given the church

9 Amy Hollingsworth,*The Simple Faith of Mr. Rogers* (Thomas Nelson Publishing, April 6, 2012).

with which to conquer evil, and that always assumes that we know how to use the keys.

Elizabeth Bishop told a beautiful story in her poem titled *The Fish*[10]. She says she caught a great big fish that looked battered and homely and she held it beside the boat half out of the water. She looked at him gasping for air, his eyes shifting back and forth, and then she noticed his lower lip was grim and wet with five old pieces of fishing line, and all five hooks had grown firmly into his mouth. He had escaped five times but now she had him dead to rights. She stared at her victory while all around the rented boat, the oil escaping from a rusted engine spread a rainbow in the water, and when she saw that rainbow, she just let him go. She set him free.

I pray the church, when it encounters people with failures in their lives, will remember that rainbow and take the keys Jesus gave us and set them free. That's how Jesus used the keys, and that's why he gave them to us. Grace isn't one of the things we are. It is *the* thing we are.

---

10 Elizabeth Bishop, *The Complete Poems* (Farrar, Straus an Girox, New York), 42-44.

Chapter Three

What God Expects From The Preacher

As a beginning preacher in the early '70s, I used to search for what I would preach next. I can remember thinking, "I preached on God's love last week; I must choose something else this week," and I hunted through the Bible for topics to preach. Many preachers do that every single week, an exhaustive search for something new and different. Unfortunately, as well intentioned as that exercise may be, it is not the calling of the preacher.

Preachers are ordained to the gospel ministry, which means searching for ways to preach the good news of God's love from any text and every text. Good news is good news. That doesn't vary from week to week.

When a preacher stands in the pulpit, he or she is commissioned to speak a good word for God. The first step to becoming a good preacher is to remember that. The sermon is *always about God.* As we said earlier, when we attempt to talk about us… there goes the good news.

Again, I remember in my first church the lady saying to me, "I don't feel like I've been to church unless the preacher has stepped on my toes." I hope that poor soul got some help, because anyone who comes to church for that reason needs some serious therapy.

The very real fact is that people come to church carrying a variety of burdens. Over here is someone battling crippling arthritis, on the other side of the room sits one that is undergoing radiation and chemotherapy, up front is someone facing a frightening surgical procedure, and all through the room the heavy burdens go. Someone is dealing with smothering grief. Another person is suffering from enormous guilt and remorse. Someone is going through trouble with their marriage, and another is dealing with a painful divorce. Still another is wrestling with unresolved anger. There are a hundred different "sacks of rocks" carried into every worship service, and what people need is the good news of God's love and care and sustaining grace. The preacher does well to remember that their number one responsibility is to deliver that good news.

Occasionally, there is one for whom life is going by as smooth as silk at the present, but their day is coming. No one can have the gospel reinforced into their reservoir too much. Every single worship service is a rehearsal for what is coming around the corner. Therefore, no preacher should assume that they are dwelling on love, forgiveness, and hope too much. Every Christian needs the reassurance that the one who chose to bring them into the world can be counted on to give them what they need when they most need it, because that's how grace always comes… when we need it.

We hear the good news in church, often *before* we need it, and we cannot yet hear it. I once read a line that has stayed with me through the years. The line was this: "Since we can't let the good news into our hearts, we place the words of hope on top of our hearts and may not even know they are there." But those holy words are there, and they stay there until one day our hearts break, and the words fall in. I believe that's a good description of worship as rehearsal for life. If people have no need of the gospel at present, they will be thankful they have it in a savings account for the day that they will need it.

Ancient Hebrews thought of the rainbow as God's promise of presence and care. Christians depend on the preaching of the gospel as that promise. It's the responsibility of every preacher to provide it, not occasionally, but every single Sunday and there are a thousand good ways to express it.

Let me share another story from Tom Long about a woman in South Carolina whose name was Ruth. She lived in a little shack outside a small town. She was the equivalent of what is called "a street person." She used to go into a grocery store every morning about 11:00 a.m. and make her way through the aisles. There is no polite way to describe what she did. She stole food. Every morning, she stole enough food for one good meal a day.

She put pieces of fruit, a load of bread, a wedge of cheese, or a can of meat under her torn and stained coat, and then walked out the door. But they knew what she was doing. They saw her doing it. The stock boys saw it. The butcher saw it. The checkout clerks were aware of the food under her coat, as she left the store each day. The manager knew she was doing it.

Several months later, the grocery store moved several blocks closer into town and into a larger building, and the week they moved, the manager telephoned a pastor nearby and said, "I don't want to embarrass Ruth, so would you please find her and tell her where we moved? I want to be sure she can find us."[11] It's a remarkable story about mercy, a mercy that should appeal to all preachers.

I remember one of the members of a church I served, who said to me when her husband died of alcoholism, "I'm afraid he didn't go to heaven." There was no consoling her. She believed you had to climb a ladder of good works into heaven and staying drunk was not one of them. I tried to explain the grace of God to her, but she wasn't having any of it, so I opened her Bible to John 3:16 and asked her to read it. When she had read it, I asked her, "Does that say anything about drinking or not drinking?" She said, "No." That seemed to calm her fears. Preachers are commissioned to do that every Sunday, to calm fears with the gospel of Christ. If a preacher would rather enforce the law, he or she should become a policeman.

When Jesus said, "Follow me," it meant he was going somewhere and wanted to take us with him. But there are pitfalls along the way, and many lose their way and must be found. That's what the gospel does. It finds people who have lost their way, even though they are Christians. Nobody is perfect, especially the ones who think they are.

The leader of the disciples, Simon Peter, lost his way. In an hour of Jesus' greatest need, Peter denied even knowing him, let alone following him. He was so ashamed that he left his mission and went back to fishing.

11 Sermon delivered by Dr. Tom Long

He felt disqualified to serve Jesus any longer. He completely lost his way. Jesus found him out on the Sea of Galilee, and while the others swam in to see Jesus, Simon dog-paddled as long as he could, because he was afraid of facing the music. But when he finally came to shore, Jesus found his wayward sheep and brought him back into the fold.

Jonah is yet another example of one who lost his way. God told him to go to Nineveh to preach to Israel's enemy, in what today is Iraq. Jonah wanted no part of that and took a ship in the opposite direction. But after an unpleasant experience with a storm, some irate sailors and a whale, the Bible says, "The word of the Lord came to Jonah a second time." What that is saying is that God was serious about giving the Assyrians another chance, so much so that God gave Jonah another chance.

God has always made a priority of finding those who have lost their way. All through the Bible that is true. Jesus called himself "the Good Shepherd" for a reason. He spoke of a shepherd who would leave 99 to fend for themselves while he searched for one that was lost, and when he found it, he didn't punish it or scold it. He picked it up and put it on his own strong shoulders and brought it back into the fold. It didn't mean the shepherd didn't love the 99, but that he loved each one of the hundred, individually. Every one of the sheep was that important.

In the gospel of John (10:11-18), Jesus reiterated what the prophet Ezekiel (34:11-16a) had spoken of earlier: God in Christ is the good shepherd, the kind that takes ownership of his sheep. He doesn't disown them because they have strayed. He doesn't leave them when they leave him. He comes to find them. They are his own. They are marked as his forever.

Jesus didn't teach that God loves us because we are good sheep. God loves us because God is the Good Shepherd and the Good Shepherd believes that love and forgiveness will bring about repentance. It doesn't work the other way around. That was the Pharisee's position. "Repent and you'll be accepted." But with the Good Shepherd it is "You are accepted," and that causes people to repent. The Pharisees' position is a religion of law, but the position of Jesus is a religion of grace.

He believed in the Good Shepherd concept so much that he was willing to die for it. It shows us God's hope never dies, God's love never stops, and God's mercy never ceases. No matter who we are or what we've done, the Good Shepherd will find us. There is no image in the Bible more reassuring than that of the Good Shepherd and his sheep.

I can remember sitting in my study one day years ago, when I received a phone call telling me that a teenage girl had been killed in a motorcycle accident. The hospital was calling to ask if I would like to notify the next of kin, because they were members of my church. That was a daunting task to be sure, but that's not the worst of it. As it so happened, ten years before, the same couple had been contacted to notify them that their teenage son had been killed in a car accident. They were receiving this terrible news twice, and both of their children were only sixteen years old at the time of their deaths.

You can only imagine how much I dreaded being the bearer of this bad news. It was just more than anyone should have to hear in a lifetime. As I made my way down the steps to my car, I thought to myself, "What kind of an awful world is this, that something like this can happen twice to the same couple? It's just unbelievable! It's unjust. It's not right." I said a prayer out loud in my car, "Dear God, I think you ought to have to go yourself and make this visit! This world of yours is disgusting!"

Sometime later I told John Carlton, my mentor, what had happened, how I had responded in anger, and how I was still struggling with it. He said, "What if that was God crying out in you, Jack, about the injustice that happened to his children, deep calling unto deep, expressing it through you? You don't really believe you came up with that yourself, do you? It was the Good Shepherd in you crying out in pain, and it was the Good Shepherd going to that house. You didn't go alone."

The Good Shepherd always cares, always loves, and *always* finds us. Today's preacher should see their task as God's agent for finding those who have lost their way or need God's care, and the best way to do that, week to week, is by preaching the gospel and assuring people of the grace of God.

Most people have heard of "Wrong Way Riegels." In the 1929 Rose Bowl, Georgia Tech was playing California, when a player named Riegels recovered a fumble for California and ran 65 yards in the wrong direction. His mistake ended up costing his team a safety that ended the first half.

When Coach Nibs Price came into the dressing room at halftime, he made no mention of what happened. He simply said, "The team that started the game will start the second half." All the players headed back onto the field, except Riegels. He just kept sitting there, head in his hands, crying, embarrassed, and humiliated. He was inconsolable.

That's when Coach Price came over to him and said, "Riegels, go out there and try again, son. There's still another half to play." But Riegels couldn't hear the grace, because he wouldn't forgive himself. He said, "Coach, I can't do it. I don't deserve to go back out there. I've disgraced you, disgraced my school, and disgraced myself. I couldn't face that crowd out there to save my life."

Coach Price put his hand on Riegels' shoulder and said, "Roy, deserve's got nothing to do with it. I'm still the coach, and I said the game is only half over. Now get out there and play."

He went back out onto the field, and the other players said they had never seen anyone play as hard as he played the second half. He accepted the grace he was given, and it brought about repentance. To this day, he's still known as "Wrong Way Riegels," which is just like humans to remember failures, but that's not what Coach Price did. From that day forward, he always called him, "Second Half Riegels."[12] That's who God is, that's what God is like, and that's the message of any preacher of the gospel. It is the high calling of ministry.

Preachers of the gospel have all kinds of opportunities to share the good news. During my seminary days I served a marvelous church in the Raleigh area, in a kind of internship. I was the associate pastor and minister to youth at First Baptist Church of Clayton, North Carolina.

Susie Powell was one of our youth. But Susie wasn't able to come

12 Sermon by Dr. Dillard Mynatt

to church with the other youth. She suffered from cystic fibrosis. It was 1972, before they could do very much about the disease at all. It affected both the respiratory and digestive systems of a patient. I visited Susie regularly in her home, often finding her under an oxygen tent. I used to take her Nancy Drew mysteries, because she liked to read, and they were just right for a girl her age confined to her home. I asked her on one occasion, "Susie, what would you like to do, if you could only do it?" Her answer was, "I'd like to be able to eat a peanut butter sandwich," and I am certain the angels of heaven blushed at the simplicity of her wish.

We had plenty of time to talk on my frequent visits, and I became more and more comfortable with our conversations, as I got to know her. When I graduated from seminary and moved to my first parish in Tennessee, I had to say goodbye to Susie, a very difficult parting for me and for her. Not long after I arrived at my new church, I received a phone call from Susie's mother. She said, "Jack, we are at Duke Hospital and Susie is dying." My heart stood still when I heard those words. After a few seconds her mother said, "She asked me to call you, Jack. She is dying, and she wants to know... what it's like to die."

Now, what do you say? A little girl, just thirteen years old, afraid, wants to ask you what it's like to die. But because of the words of grace I had heard or read from competent teachers and preachers, I could recall a story I didn't even know was there. It had been on my heart and now it fell into my heart.

When Susie came on the phone I said, "Susie, have you ever been in the car with your folks, and you were in the backseat asleep, and your daddy carried you in the house and put you in your bed, and you woke up the next day in your own room?" She said, "Yes." I said, "It will be just like that, honey, just like that." And she said, "Thank you, Jack." I said, "I love you. God is with you, right there by your side." And we hung up.

The need for the gospel comes, and when it comes, there is no greater responsibility or greater privilege than to be the one who shares it. That can only happen if the gospel is the main thing that gets you up in the morning and sends you through another day. My appeal to any minister, of any age, is to see to it, so help you God, that the gospel is the main thing for you, your north star, your guiding light, and the very breath that you breathe. That is the medicine you will share with those you serve.

Chapter Four

The Work Of Grace In The Human Heart

When someone leans toward a religion of law, they often point out the fact that Jesus said, "I did not come to destroy the law but to fulfill it." Let's look at that verse for a moment. What does it mean to fulfill something? It means bringing it to completion. The law, void of the grace of Jesus Christ, is without mercy and therefore incomplete. It puts more emphasis on the law than the people God loves. But when Jesus came bringing the grace of God, the law now had its missing ingredient, which was mercy. The law was now fulfilled.

When the Pharisees criticized Jesus' disciples for plucking grain on the sabbath, Jesus told them, "If you knew what the scripture 'I desire mercy and not sacrifice means,' you would not have criticized my disciples." Do you see what was missing? It was law without mercy. Jesus' concern was for the people for whom the law was given, and not the law itself. Pharisees of any era just don't understand this. They think if something is in the Bible, it must be correct.

But the law of Jesus' day justified violence, slavery, the suppression of women, and murderous prejudice against gay people. If you baptize the law with the grace and mercy of Jesus' gospel, it is okay to say, "We don't believe those things anymore. They have been fulfilled, updated, and tempered by mercy." Law doesn't appear in our Bibles to say, "God wanted all this." It appears there so that we might see how people behaved before Jesus, and so we might see the change he has brought about.

Christian theology teaches us that there are two main ways God reveals God's self. The first way is called "general revelation," and includes such things as nature, poetry, music, inspired prose, the stars, the ocean, and even lessons taught in movies. The Bible belongs in this kind of revelation. It is an inspired book, written over many centuries, and has always put people in touch with God. It is like a great window through which God reveals God's self.

What if you had a house on the ocean, and you took some friends to enjoy the spacious view of the sea through your very large picture window? What would you think if, instead of commenting on the marvelous view, they commented on the window? "My, what a lovely window this is! What kind of glass is this made of? Oh, here's a smudge. Give me something to clean this, because this window is perfect. It is without error." You wanted them to look through the window at the view beyond it, and all they could do was deify the window! Some people do that with the Bible. It is a means through which to see God. It is not God itself.

The other kind of revelation is "special revelation." Special revelation is the revelation of God in Jesus Christ. The church has long said that anyone who puts a general revelation ahead of the special revelation is guilty of idolatry.

It is in the revelation of God in Jesus that we get our greatest picture of who God is and what God is doing in the world, and it is in the life of Jesus that we see the embodiment of the gospel. That same gospel is visible in a person, occasionally. It is hope for the rest of us of what we can yet be. God is not finished with us yet.

Grace, grateful, and gracious all come from the same root word. As grace flows through us, it evokes gratitude to God for his kindness, mercy, and care, and to be grateful is to become gracious. They are interconnected, and that's how grace does its work in the human heart.

It is the secret to feeling forgiven. Often, people say, "I believe that God forgives me, but I don't feel forgiven." I tell them, "Forgive someone. Let forgiveness flow through you, and then you will feel forgiven." The ancient mystics, when they were asked, "Whose sin is forgiven, answered, "The sin of the ones who forgave a sin committed against them." It is the deepest meaning behind the Lord's Prayer, when it says, "Forgive us our trespasses, *as we forgive those* who trespass against us." It is as forgiveness flows through us that we, ourselves, feel forgiven. Forgiveness really is like soap. Soap must flow through a cloth. It doesn't clean a cloth just to pour soap *on* a cloth. Grace received is meant to be grace shared, and none of us can store grace just for ourselves.

Most of us don't think of ourselves as the worst people in town. We can find plenty of others, who have more for which to be forgiven, and because of that we don't have the gratitude that others may have and may not be as gracious and forgiving. Indeed, you can't be too bad for God to forgive you, but you can be too good for forgiveness to ever flow through you.

If you should be tempted to say, "I just cannot ever forgive what he did. It's too great. I could never forgive it in a million years." Could that be because you haven't been forgiven for much in your own life? The more you are forgiven, the more grateful you will be, and the more grateful you are, the more gracious and forgiving you can become. Consequently, the reverse is true.

Jesus once had dinner at the home of Simon the Pharisee. A woman of the street entered the house, uninvited, and began to weep at the feet of Jesus. Simon was infuriated. "Why is this man having anything to do with a woman like her? It shows he's not a prophet." And Jesus said, "She has been forgiven much, Simon, and she is grateful. You have not been forgiven much, and you are not as grateful."

Harry Pritchett is the former rector of St. John's Cathedral in New York. He now lives in Atlanta. I invited him to speak to a group of ministers at a retreat in Gatlinburg. He told us the story of a man, who came to him late one evening, as he was leaving the cathedral. The man said, "Please say a prayer for me and ask God to forgive my sin."

Harry said, "What is your name?" The man replied, "Silver DaRancho," and Harry thought, "That's a made-up name if I ever heard one." But he prayed for the man anyway. He said, "Holy Father, please allow your servant, Silver DaRancho, to know that you still love him, that you forgive him, that you cleanse him from his sin and set him free by the love of your precious blood. Amen."

When he finished, the man said, "Pray for me again. You see, I'm an actor, and Silver DaRancho is my stage name. I want you to use my real name this time." And they prayed together again and used his real name.[13] And Harry told all of us who were present at the retreat, "God knows the real you, not the one you pretend to be, and God still loves you and forgives you and those in the congregation you serve."

It is good to know that the final work of grace in the human heart is not just about going to heaven when you die. The final work of grace is to make us grateful and gracious.

Several years ago, I read an article about wild geese that was most interesting, since geese live all around me on a nearby lake. The article pointed out that geese were made to fly in formation. They do much better in formation than when they fly alone. The article said that they take turns in leadership and honk encouragement to one another as they travel. All along the way, they care for those who fall and are wounded. Some of them will stay with a crippled or injured bird in the snow, even though it will cost them their lives.

When they fly, it is always with their heads up, pointed to the horizon. They never look down. When I read all that I thought, "Not just geese, but people are made to be like that." It's the work of grace in the human heart to encourage those who lead, to care for those who've fallen, and to keep our heads up with hope. That is the transformation that grace makes possible in you and me.

Richard Wing said, when he was a young minister, he was talking to a mechanic friend that was working on his car. Richard told him that he would like to take the gospel to different places and help start new churches, but his mechanic said, "Your job is right here, Richard, right here where God has put you. Your job is to go and find light in people. You aren't set up to judge anybody, just to find light in the rottenest people. You never know how much light is buried deep in a rotten guy. It may be buried under pain and guilt and the condemnation of others.

13 Harry Pritchett, Mynatt Ministers Retreat, Gatlinburg, Tennessee

Your job is to peel off that junk and find the light in them. Everybody's got some light, Richard. Some may have only a little and it's buried deep, but it's your job to find it."[14]

Richard said he found the voice of God in the voice of that mechanic, and he went back to his church with a new focus and a new energy. The grace of God came to him through another human being.

I have found great grace in Psalm 121. It is a psalm that reminds us that God can be trusted, if we will trust God one moment at a time. You can't do it in advance. You trust from moment to moment. The psalmist said God doesn't doze — he doesn't sit in a recliner and doze off. You don't have to be afraid in the daytime or in the middle of the night. God is with you. God will keep you. He will keep your going out and your coming in.

Think of all the "going outs" and "coming ins" we experience in a lifetime. There is the time we leave home and start to school, the time we move from grade to grade, the time for graduation, the time to go to college or to find work, or the time to be married, or change jobs and locations, and to undergo anesthetics for surgeries. All those times involve going out and coming in. Even death itself is a going out and a coming in, and the psalmist says, "Don't be afraid. God will keep your going out and coming in."

God's grace always calms our fears. The first gospel sermon ever preached was from angels to shepherds in their fields, and the message was, "Fear not, we have some good news."

Angelo Roncalli, better known as Pope John XXIII, was involved in some of the most sweeping changes in the history of the Roman Catholic Church. He was the first pope to refer to protestants as "separated brethren." Always ecumenical, he was full of the grace of God. When Angelo became pope he said, "We're going to open the windows of the church and let in some fresh air," and when you've been graced and become gracious like that, there is always opposition. He lived in constant stress, but this is what he would pray before he went to bed

14 Sermon delivered by Richard Wing

at night: "Who governs the church, Angelo? You? Or God? Very well, then, go to sleep, Angelo. Go to sleep."[15] That is the work of grace in the human heart. And that's what the psalmist is talking about in Psalm 121.

John Claypool was fond of sharing a story about his friend, Reuel Howe, a hospital chaplain in New Orleans. Reuel was visiting a friend in the hospital, who was dying, and his friend said, "I'm not afraid, Reuel." So Reuel said, "Tell me about your wonderful trust. Surely it is the work of grace in your heart."

The man said, "Every exit I've ever taken has always been an entrance on the other side. If you walk out a door, you're coming in somewhere else. All through my life, I have given up something to gain something. I believe death is just an old friend in a new garb. It's leaving something you love for something greater."

Not long after that, Reuel's friend died and Reuel conducted the funeral service. At the conclusion, as they were going out to the hearse, Reuel looked up at the sign over the door and it said, E-X-I-T, and he remembered what his friend had said. The work of grace in a human heart produces that kind of trust. The preaching of God's grace makes Christians *more* Christian. A deeper trust takes years to develop, and that growth is the product of a steady diet of the gospel.

15 Lecture delivered by Dr. John W. Carlton

Chapter Five

Times When Grace Is Needed Most

There are times in the lives of all of us when an abundance of grace is needed to get us through a difficult hour. The ancient Hebrews found grace when they came to the Red Sea place in their own lives.

Six hundred thousand people approached the banks of the Red Sea with pharaoh's troops in hot pursuit. They couldn't go back. They couldn't go around. They had no choice but to go right through the sea, trusting the grace of God.

All of us come to those "Red Sea places" in our lives, and when we do, we find that we are not alone there. God is there too, to help us through our Red Sea. God is at every Red Sea. It could be a time of great suffering or of smothering grief. It could be a time when an act of forgiveness is the only way through a great disappointment and betrayal. It could be any time of decision.

Carlyle Marney was the senior minister at Myers Park Baptist Church in Charlotte. He says he had a dream for his church. His dream was that on Monday morning, when the janitor came in to collect the trash and sweep it out of the sanctuary, he would find more than someone's umbrella, some chewing gum wrappers, a couple of Bibles, and someone's glasses.

His dream was that the janitor would find someone's grief, a bitter disappointment, someone's failure and guilt, another person's bitter hurt, still another person's painful pride, and someone's greatest fears. He dreamed all of that could be swept out of his church on Monday morning. Those are all Red Sea places. They remind us that we can plunge into our own Red Sea and leave all that debris behind, because God will make the way through for us.

Shirley Guthrie taught theology at Columbia Seminary in Atlanta.

He wrote a wonderful layperson's book of theology that is very readable. It's called simply *Christian Doctrine.* He spent his entire life teaching people about God.

One day he learned that he was dying of cancer. He was under hospice care and many of his colleagues and students came to visit him. A friend was with him one day near the end of his life, when he said, "You know, I've spent my whole life teaching people about God. And now I know it's true." The grace of God got Shirley Guthrie through his Red Sea. It always does.

Mark described our pilgrimage in this life as being in a boat with Jesus, on our way to the "other side." Some of us will get there sooner than others, but all of us are on our way to the other side. But Mark says being in the boat with Jesus is not a smooth ride. The disciples encountered a heavy storm when they rode with Jesus, and it wasn't because they were disobedient. It was because they were very obedient. They were doing what Jesus instructed them to do.

A lot of people think when storms come into their lives they are being punished. They ask, "Why is this happening to me? I have tried to do what Jesus wants me to do." But that has nothing to do with the storms. The storms come to us because we are human, and they are a part of what it means to be human.

But the first disciples were afraid that Jesus didn't care about what was happening to them. In fact, they asked him, "Don't you care?" Jesus stilled their storm. His grace is very powerful and filled with our best interest at heart. And when Jesus stilled their storm, he said, "Why are you guys afraid? Why would you think I don't care? Why would you doubt that I could help you?" Mark knows we have fears, but he wants to put that fear to rest, and that's what the story of the storm at sea is all about. He wants us all to know that when the storms come, God's grace is sufficient to get us through them. They are Red Sea experiences, and we can plunge right in with God at our side.

Paul taught the same thing. When he wrote the Corinthian church, he told them about a painful condition in his life that he referred to as

38

his "thorn in the flesh." He told them he prayed three times about it, and this was God's reply. "My grace is sufficient for you, for my power is made perfect in weakness." In other words, my grace comes when you need it most.

Once when I was leaving one church to accept another, I remember a conversation with a man in the church I was leaving. He lived alone. He had no family, and I had become particularly close to him. I was convinced it was for just such people that Jesus came into the world. He always attended every single service of the church and never failed to express his appreciation for any of them.

He was kind and thoughtful, and had come to depend on me in many ways, so I singled him out, before I told the church. I wanted him to know first of my decision to leave. I knew it would hurt him, and I wanted to reassure him. I said, "This is something I just have to do," and with tears in his eyes he said, "I know. I respect that. I believe God will be with you, Jack, and God will be with me. And God will be with both of our churches."

I was going to comfort him, but he comforted me. It was strength from heaven sufficient for the moment, and as we walked outside the church into the parking lot, there appeared the biggest, brightest rainbow I have ever seen. The rainbow has long been a sign of hope that God will love us and care for us forever and seeing that rainbow was a visible reminder to me of God's sustaining grace.

No one can say how God will provide the grace you need, when you most need it. We can only say God will provide it. You can count on that. It is the Bible's hope that you and I will cling to grace in such a way as to graciously share it with others, just as my friend did for me.

One of Paul's greatest disappointments in life came when the church at Galatia moved away from this kind of grace and replaced it once again with law. He wrote them a painful letter and says, "You've fallen away from grace. You are no longer practicing grace." They had left the gospel and gone back to Orthodox Judaism.

Paul was very upset with these people. He asked them, "Do you remember what got you started as a Christian? Remember when I taught you that God so loved the world that he sent his son, not just to Bible believers, but to the whole world? Do you remember that? Whatever happened to that? You've changed it into Bible interpretation. Who changed you to be like that? You are a people who have received the grace of God, and a people meant to extend the grace of God to others."

Let me tell you of one couple who shared grace with me. Their names were Dick and Mary Helen Woodard, and they were members of my seminary intern church. I was five hundred miles from home, as the song goes, and I was learning how to serve. I learned as much in that church in a practical nature, as I learned at seminary in an academic nature.

Dick had an Amoco Station, and I always bought my gas and changed my oil there. I learned about hospitality from Dick. I learned about generosity from Dick and Mary Helen. I learned what it was like to be treated like family, when I wasn't even family. Routinely, Dick would invite me over to his house for lunch after Sunday morning worship. I had never seen such food in all my life, always two meats, roast beef and pork loin — or fried chicken and pork barbecue.

Mary Helen would ask, "Which would you like, Jack?" And Dick would quickly say, "Give him some of both!" The vegetables were the best eastern North Carolina had to offer: field peas and butter beans, corn and okra, green beans and mashed potatoes, sweet potatoes and watermelon pickles. The table was filled with those things.

Mary Helen would ask, "What can I pass you, Jack?" And Dick would say, "Give him some of all of 'em." Every time I visited their home, I was reminded of what God told Adam and Eve in the Garden of Eden. "If you eat of it all, you shall surely die."

But the food was not the only reason I loved to visit at Dick's and Mary Helen's. I knew I was loved there. I knew I was accepted there. It was pure grace to be with them.

The Bible tells of one who experienced such a grace. His name is not one you hear every day. No mother names her son after him. His name was Mephibosheth. He was Jonathan's son, King Saul's grandson. They had dropped him when he was a baby, and it injured his leg so badly that he was crippled and couldn't walk.

They had hidden him after his father and grandfather were killed in battle, for fear that the new king, in this case David, would kill any remaining members of the former king's family to prevent them from ever challenging for the throne. When David asked if there were any remaining family members in Saul's household, it must have struck fear in the ears of those who heard it.

But David didn't ask in order that he might kill them. He said, "I want to show God's kindness to that person." David's servants searched and found Mephibosheth, and they brought him to the king's palace. The frightened and crippled young man bowed his face on the floor and said, "I am your servant."

David said, "Don't be afraid. I will be kind to you for your father, Jonathan's sake, and I'm going to give you back all the land of your grandfather, Saul, and you'll always eat at my table." From that day, Mephibosheth was treated as if he were one of David's own sons. He was made a prince again, a part of the royal family, and David always referred to him as "son."

Mephibosheth experienced the grace of God through David, and David did this because he believed in God's incredible grace, that God knew how we were made and remembers that we are dust. Those who have received grace, like David, are meant to be bearers of grace when it is needed most.

Back in the 1950s and '60s, people who lived on the seacoast of southern Florida were always intrigued by a ritual they saw repeated every night of the week. As the sun went down, they would see an old man with a bucket of live shrimp standing on a pier feeding seagulls. The man's name was Eddie Rickenbacker, the most celebrated war hero of World War 1. When the second world war broke out, he was called back into service, and while he was flying his B17 over the Pacific he became lost, ran out of fuel, and had to ditch the airplane. Seven members of his

41

crew lived on life rafts for 23 days.

They had enough drinking water with them but their rations disappeared quickly, so they grew weaker and weaker. Late one evening as the sun went down, Rickenbacker lay down and pulled his hat over his face and tried to go to sleep, when something utterly amazing happened. A seagull landed on his head, and that bird gave up its life that those men might live. They used parts of the seagull for bait to catch enough fish to be able to survive those 23 days until they were rescued.

When the war ended, Rickenbacker retired to south Florida, where every evening for twenty years he did the same thing. As the sun went down, he got a bucket of shrimp and went to the pier and fed the very birds that twenty years earlier had saved his life.

He said, "It's my way of expressing gratitude to a grace I cannot begin to understand. To this day, nobody can tell me how that seagull got so far out into the Pacific, but I want to be as generous to creation as years ago creation was generous to me."[16]

---

16 Max Lucado, *In the Eyes of the Storm* (Nashville, TN; Thomas Nelson Press. 2012) 221, 225-226.

Chapter 6

Clothe Yourselves In Love

In his letter to the Colossians (3:14), Paul gave us the secret to receiving and sharing the grace of God. He said, "Clothe yourselves in love." When you've sinned, when you're weak, when you're afraid, and when you wish to forgive someone… clothe yourselves in love. That is how grace comes, and that's how grace is shared. After Paul's persecution of Christians that even resulted in the death of some of them, what if he had just clothed himself in shame? That was Judas' mistake. You can be no good to anyone if you clothe yourself in shame. Clothe yourself in love, and God's forgiveness can make its way through you. Moses had to do that. David had to do that. Simon Peter had to do that after denying Jesus.

The way to live after failure is always to clothe ourselves in the love of God. The love of God even allows you to forgive yourself. Grace comes to people who clothe themselves with the love of God.

The desert monastics tell some wonderful stories. One of them is the story of how one of the monks was called before the council. The council called upon their leader to preside over their brother's judgment. The leader agreed to come, but to make his point, he took a jug with a leak in it, filled it with water, and carried it with him into the meeting.

The monks said, "What is this?" Their leader said, "My sins run out behind me, and I don't even see them. Yet, you ask me to judge the sin of someone else?" When they heard these words, the council voted to forgive their brother. Those who clothe themselves with the love of God simply cannot judge another person. It becomes impossible.

Jeremiah told us that God is like a potter at his wheel. When something he has made is flawed, he puts it back on the wheel and reshapes it into something better. He isn't finished with it just because it is flawed.

Here we all are, forgiven and in need of forgiveness, and there is God's love and forgiveness. Paul would surely ask us, "What are you waiting for?" Put it on! It's yours! Put it on!"

In the same letter, Paul said it was the love of Christ in us that gives us hope. He calld it "the hope of glory," and it means the uninterrupted presence of God. Paul knew the closeness that we all seek can fade. The secret to the grace we so desperately need is Christ in us. When Christ is within you, you will remember that Christ is for you. People worry about that frequently.

One woman, after her husband died on a hunting trip asked me, "Do you think he was all right with God? He believed in God. He trusted God, but he didn't come to church. Do you think he's in heaven?" I said, "I think he went right into the hands of the Good Shepherd, who found him and took him home."

The hope she wanted could have been found in the Christ within her. It is something we have to remember. When Jesus lives within you, he always gives you hope. It just takes remembering he is with you.

I remember one old gentleman in McMinn County, Tennessee. His name was George Putnam, and he was in his nineties. Christ was so present in this man, and he spoke with such kindness, wisdom, and mercy that all the workers at the nursing home where he stayed went to him with their problems.

And you know something? So did I! I went to visit him many times, but it was he who visited me. The love of Christ within him not only gave him hope, Christ within him gave us all hope! He knew Christ was for him, and he never went back to the starting point to ask that question again.

In the book of Acts, Luke told of a man who found hope in the life of one who was clothed in love. We don't know the man's name that needed hope. Luke told us he was a eunuch from Ethiopia. In his culture, polygamy was practiced, and men sometimes had harems of wives numbering into the hundreds. They considered their wives to be property and were very jealous and protective of them. They would take

44

prisoners of war and turn them into slaves that they put in charge of taking care of all their wives. But they could do this only after they had been rendered surgically sexless, against their will, of course. This injustice had happened to this man.

Somewhere, in his many travels, this eunuch had heard of the Hebrew faith, and its monotheism was very appealing to him, compared to the many gods that were worshiped where he lived, so he set out to learn more about Judaism. But when he visited the temple in Jerusalem, he was not allowed to set his foot inside. He was a gentile and a eunuch — and hated on both counts. Jews especially hated eunuchs.

They couldn't father children, and the Hebrews were a small nation, who were conquered many times because of it, and were specifically instructed to be fruitful and multiply. Therefore, they were very prejudiced against those who could not have children. That hatred included eunuchs, homosexuals, and even women who could not conceive. They were called "barren women," and Hebrew scriptures reflect their feelings about all those who could not bear children.

This man, who had suffered someone else's abuse, was now the victim of the abuse of the Judaism of his day, the very people who talked about doing justly and loving mercy and walking humbly with God. Alas, much of this hatred has been passed down to the church, and most don't even know how it originated.

Because he is rejected at the temple, this man is forced to try to understand the Hebrew scriptures on his own. That's when he met up with Philip, a deacon and an instrument of grace, clothed in love. Philip knew God was no respecter of persons and that God loved everyone, even those the Hebrews condemned.

Philip explained the scriptures to the eunuch, who then asked him, "What prevents me from being baptized?" It's a curious question. He had been prevented from entering the temple, so he naturally assumed that the church of that day would prevent him from being a part of Christianity as well. But Philip told him that nothing whatsoever prevented his acceptance, and he baptized him then and there. Many of today's church do not neccessarily agree with Philip's decision.

The reason this is a curious passage in Christian scripture is because the very act of baptism, meant to include converts into the Christian faith, is today used as a reason to prevent people from entering some churches, because of their mode of baptism. It seems that people of every age and every religion have the need to exclude certain people, when their only real calling is to *include*. What is done today in many churches is the same thing that happened to this man, when he tried to enter the Jewish temple. People are still finding reasons for exclusion.

It is a warm and heartening thing that God has always had people like Philip, who were people of grace in an otherwise graceless institution. There is no greater gift Christians can give than the gift of grace, the gift of forgiveness, and the gift of hope.

On the night of April 4, 1968, Robert Kennedy was to deliver a campaign speech in Indianapolis but shortly before he was to speak, he learned of Martin Luther King's murder in Memphis. Some thought he should cancel his speech. Other aides thought he should go ahead with it. But Kennedy did neither. Instead, on the dark, dark Thursday night, he stood before a mainly black audience and told them of King's death.

Then he delivered the speech of his life, not the one he had planned. He told the crowd, "I know what it's like to lose someone to murder. My brother was killed by a white man. But what we need in the United States is not division, not hatred, not violence, but love and wisdom and compassion toward one another. We need a feeling of justice towards those who still suffer within our country, whether they be white or black."

He quoted the Greek poet, Aeschylus, who said, "Even in our sleep, pain which cannot forget falls drop by drop upon the heart, until in our own despair, against our will, comes wisdom through the awful (awe-filled in today's language) grace of God." He closed by encouraging the crowd, "Let's dedicate ourselves to what the Greeks wrote so many years ago: 'To take the savageness of man, and to make gentle the life of this world.' Pray for our country and our people."[17]

Rather than exploding in rage at the tragic news of King's death, which happened throughout the country, this crowd dispersed quietly, surprised by the awe-filled grace of God that appeared in a politician at a desperate time. Philip and Robert are but two examples of what the Christian church and its preachers are called to be. There is abundant room for more carriers of God's grace and for those clothed in God's love. The difference it can make in someone else's life is astounding.

On the other hand, there is a painful example of the hoarding of grace in a parable Jesus once told about a Jewish wedding (Matthew 25:1-13). In those days, weddings sometimes lasted for an entire week, and the crowning event was not the appearance of the bride, but the arrival of the groom! The groom was the last to appear at those weddings, and bridesmaids of that day had to be sure they had enough oil in their lamps for the groom's appearance. But alas, some of the bridesmaids did not save enough oil. They were unprepared and missed the wedding celebration.

It is sad that these girls were not going to be a part of all that fun. And it's sad that the groom doesn't recognize them in this parable. He is often spoken of allegorically as representing Jesus, but I don't think so. Jesus recognized latecomers. One of them died on the cross beside him.

Hank Thompson was a star of the Grand Ole Opry in the early 1950's, and years after he had retired, he decided to return back to Nashville to see the Opry and to go backstage afterward. The guards, who were much younger, said "Hold on there, buddy. We don't know you." He said, "I'm Hank Thompson. I used to sing here." They said, "Sorry, we don't know you." He had to get back in his car and drive all the way back to Texas. How sad is that? It's as sad as this parable that Jesus told.

And the saddest thing of all in the parable is the lack of grace from the so-called "wise bridesmaids." When the latecomers try to borrow some oil, they say, "No, there's not enough for you and me." If there are

17 Robert Kennedy in Ray Boomhower, *Robert F. Kennedy and the 1968 Indiana Primary* (Bloomington, IN; Indiana University Press, 2008).

any words in the English language sadder than that, I don't know what they are. "Not enough for you and me."

William Barclay tried to make sense of this parable by saying, "There are some things that can't be borrowed at the last minute." Well, that's true, but oil isn't one of them! These wise girls would have been much wiser if they had been both prepared and generous. Here's an idea. Just *share* lamps. That would work.

But they say, "No." Imagine this: Suppose your ship sinks, and you end up on a desert island. There's already someone there ahead of you, and he has supplies, so you go to him for help, but he says, "Too bad, not enough for both of us." Would you like that guy?

I can remember going to school one day, when I forgot to bring something to eat at recess. Every day, we had fifteen minutes at mid-morning called recess, when we could eat some snack we brought from home. I forgot mine. Irresponsible of me I know, but I forgot. There were all kinds of snacks there. Some brought chips. Some brought candy. Others brought cookies, raisins, fruit, all kinds of things, and I didn't bring anything. I forgot it.

I said to one boy, "Can I have some of your chips?" He said, "No." I asked another boy, "Can I have one of your peanut butter crackers?" He said, "No, I'm hungry. I'll need all of them." I asked a girl seated behind me, "May I have one of your cherry cough drops?" She said, "No, you'd just want another one."

I had to sit there and do without, but the sad thing is not that I did without. I was unprepared. It was my own fault. The really sad thing was their unwillingness to help someone who was unprepared.

It happens in churches. We've all been given abundant grace from God, but we're slow to share it. I think we've all lived long enough to learn it's not easy to share the oil. I can't judge these women in the parable, because I'm guilty too. But I can question just how wise they were. They were prepared. I'll give them that. They just weren't prepared to help the unprepared. They remind me of the Pharisee who went up to the temple to pray, "Thank you, God, that I'm not like other people. I've done it right."

Many of you may remember Archie Campbell. In his autobiography, he told about the time he was a very young man. It was right after the Great Depression, and he was hungry. It was a cold winter night in Knoxville, Tennessee, when the temperature was below zero, and he began to desperately think of how he could steal some food. He knew he couldn't buy any, because he had no money. But he saw a cop standing nearby and it stopped him from breaking a window in a closed delicatessen.

His clothes were threadbare. He didn't have a coat that was warm enough for the terrible cold. His shoes were lined with cardboard where he had worn holes in the bottom of them. He went to a restaurant on Market Street that was open all night. It was called The Golden Sun, and he thought he might be allowed to stay there a few minutes, just to get out of the cold.

The man behind the counter was a man named Nick. He came over to Archie and said, "What do you want?" Archie said, "I just want to get warm, sir, if you'll let me." "Where do you live, son?" Archie just pulled a name off the top of his head. "Uh, I live at the Watauga Apartments." They were just behind the restaurant.

Nick said, "What number is your apartment?" "Uh, number one," Archie said. Nick said, "Well okay, you go over there and sit down in a booth and get warm." Archie did as he was told, and when he got warm, he fell asleep. When he awoke, Nick was putting a big breakfast in front of him. He hadn't seen that much food in days: ham and eggs, biscuits and gravy, toast and coffee. He almost cried; he was so hungry.

He said, "Sir, I couldn't give you a nickel for this meal if my life depended on it." And Nick said, "I didn't figure you could, son. And you don't live in the Watauga Apartments either, because that's where I live. I'll bet you don't even own a warm coat. You're just a kid down on your luck. Now you eat that food and rest some more. I'll wake you when it's time for the breakfast crowd to come in."

Archie said, "I have often wondered what course my life would have taken if things had gone differently that night. What if that cop hadn't been there, and I'd gone through with my plans to break into that other restaurant? What if I had not stumbled into the Golden Sun, and Nick hadn't been there with his warm heart? Years later, when I was on the Knox County School Board, kids would sometimes come before us in trouble for doing things like that, and I would be lenient on them, because I knew what a thin line separates those who go straight from those who get off the path and become lost. I knew, that in certain circumstances, getting lost could happen to just about anybody. It almost happened to me that night. There but for the grace of God go I."[18]

There are so many ways for us to share God's grace in this world. While we're waiting on the great banquet in the kingdom of God, if some foolish bridesmaid asks us if she can borrow some oil, I think we should give it to her, or at least share our lamp. Because that is the deepest meaning behind what Jesus meant when he said, "Keep awake."

Soren Kierkegaard, the Danish theologian, once commented on the words of the angels to the shepherds, as they kept their flocks by night. He said their words were, "Behold, this *day* there is born to you in the city of David, a Savior, which is Christ the Lord.

And Kierkegaard said, "It was the middle of the night! And the angels said, 'Behold this *day*.' That's always when God chooses to bring light. It always comes at the moments of our deepest darkness. That's when the light comes. God comes to us with unconditional love and mercy and gives us hope again."

I read of an interesting ordination for a minister that took place several years ago. Tom Long says that during the examination by the ordination council, one of the council members asked the candidate to look out the window and find a person walking by, any person.

The ministerial candidate said, "I see one." "Do you know that person?" "No, I don't." "Good, because what I want you to do is to describe that person for me, theologically." This man had asked that

---

18 Archie Campbell, *Archie Campbell: An Autobiography*(Memphis, TN; Memphis State University Press, 1981) 46-49.

same question of candidates for ordination for 35 years. And he had found that he usually got one of two answers.

The candidate would either say, "That person is a sinner in need of the redemptive love of God in Jesus Christ," or they would say what this young man said. He said, "Whether that person knows it or not, she is a child of God, created in God's own image and embraced by the unconditional love of God."

And the man on the council said, "Good for you, son. Good for you." He told the candidate the two answers he most often got, and he said, "Either of those answers is theologically correct. But it has been my experience, down through the years, to observe that those who give the second answer make the best ministers, because they see people through God's eyes."[19]

The church's calling and the preacher's calling is to get people to see themselves through the eyes of God's mercy, and to let God go back into all the horrible places of their lives and say, "I don't condemn you. I have come to forgive you, to save you, to find you, not to condemn you." That's the grace with which we have been entrusted. And it's shared by those who have clothed themselves in God's love and know what it is to carry God's grace.

19 Sermon delivered by Tom Long.

Chapter 7

Hope For The Individual

In 1986, the third baseman for the San Francisco Giants was Bob Brenly. In a game with the Atlanta Braves, he set a major league record by committing four errors in one game. But in his last time at bat, in the ninth inning, he hit a home run that won the game for the Giants, 7-6. That's what grace is about. With God, you have another chance to get it right, as many as it takes.

God looks at each one of us, knowing full well our darkest moments and memories, and says, "I don't condemn you. Learn from your past and learn from my forgiveness." It is the precious gift of "next time" that God gives to God's children, and it's the promise of scripture, "For I will be merciful toward their iniquities, and I will remember their sins no more," (Hebrews 8:12, a quote from Isaiah 43:25 "I am he who blots out your transgressions for my own sake, and I will not remember your sins.")

I love the story of the nun in a Catholic school, who had an "other worldly experience." She went to the priest, who was head of the school and said, "Father, I have had the most wonderful spiritual experience. I've been given a vision of God!"

The priest was skeptical, as most people are with those who have visions. He simply said, "Good for you, sister." He really thought, "Perhaps you should take a Zantac before you go to bed."

The next day, the nun came back to the priest's office and said, "It happened again, Father. It happened again! I saw a vision of God and spoke with him. It was wonderful, so reassuring!" The priest thought, "I need to get this woman some help."

On the third straight day, she came to the priest's office again, and he'd had enough. He wanted this to stop, so he devised a scheme by which to prove her wrong. He said, "The next time this happens, sister, I want you to ask God what sins I confessed last night. You tell me what they were, and I'll know you've seen God."

The very next day she came back to his office and surprised the priest by saying, "I had another vision of God, Father. It was wonderful and hopeful." The priest said, "Did you do what I told you to do? Did you ask God what sins I confessed last night?" The nun looked straight into his eyes and said, "I did, Father. I did as you told me to do." The priest said, "Well... what were they? What did God say?" And she said, "God said he didn't remember."

God's ability to forgive and forget our sins, to wipe them away forever, is the greatest gift of the gospel. It is the privilege of every preacher and every church to share that gift to a congregation in need of it. It is meant to change us.

Our opportunity for repentance is wonderful news, but often misunderstood by the church. Many still embrace the Old Testament understanding of the word, which is: Repent and God will forgive. Jesus brought a better understanding of the word, when he fulfilled the law. He brought forgiveness *before* repentance, that *brought about* the repentance of those forgiven.

There are many examples, but perhaps the most famous is the story of Zacchaeus, a tax collector Jesus accepted and forgave, and with whom he shared a meal. The result was Zacchaeus stated that he intended to give half of his possessions to the poor, and a repayment to all those he had defrauded four times greater than the money he had taken from them. Jesus said, "Today, salvation has come to this house." The Hebrew root word for salvation means "friends with God." Jesus was stating that here was a man who had restored a proper relationship with God, shown by his act of repentance. But it was Jesus' *acceptance before repentance* that brought it about. Had Jesus simply seen Zacchaeus in the crowd of people and shouted, "Repent you scoundrel, and God will forgive you," it probably would not have happened. Zacchaeus had, no doubt, heard that many times before.

True repentance begins with the knowledge that we are loved. It does not mean to confirm the little voice within you that says, "You are no good." There was a film, starring Jack Nicholson, called "As Good As It Gets." Jack plays an obsessive-compulsive neurotic with all kinds of problems, and he goes to a therapist for help. As he walks out of the psychiatrist's office in one scene, he sees all the people sitting in the waiting room and says, "What if this is as good as it gets?" Repentance is getting rid of that despair. It is realizing you are not a bad person simply because you have done a bad thing. You are not worthless and hopeless. There is the chance, with God, to make the future different from the past.

Jesus fulfilled the law by changing the people's understanding of repentance. Those they called sinners had been told by the religious authorities that they were no good, hopeless, and were forever kicked out of the synagogue to live outside God's love. But Jesus announced that God is not finished with any of us, and that God can restore and heal us. Those who heard him had to repent of the old understanding of repentance, because he taught it's not our repentance that *makes God do something*; it's God's forgiveness that *makes us do something*. Those who heard him had to change their mind and believe the good news.

To fully understand this change, think of Jesus' prayer from the cross. "Father, forgive them: for they know not what they do." You know what that is? That's forgiveness before repentance. One account says the soldier in charge of the crucifixion said, "Truly, this was the Son of God." You know what that is? It sounds like repentance. How many others there repented? We don't know. But it has changed people now for two thousand years. What if Jesus had just shouted from the cross, "Repent, you scoundrels?" Would that have done it for you?

Mary Oliver was a poet who loved dogs. One dog that came to live with her had a length of rope hanging from his collar. He played with her other dogs and then vanished. The next morning, he was back with a different rope attached. This happened for several days, the dog always accompanied by a piece of rope.

When her family moved to another house, she went back to the old house and found him lying in the grass by the door, so she put him in her car and showed him where her new house was. He stayed for a while, and then he was gone. But there he was the next morning at the new house, rope dangling.

Later that day his owner appeared with his papers and a leash. "His name is Sammy," she said, "And he's yours." Mary had a fenced in back yard, but that didn't deter Sammy. They found he could jump fences as well as he could chew ropes. He was picked up by the dog catcher on many occasions, so people began calling her to come and get him before the dog catcher found him. Some would even take him inside to hide him from the law. One woman called, and when Mary got there, she said, "Can you wait just a few minutes? I'm scrambling him some eggs." He became the mayor of all the dogs in town, and everyone loved him.

Even the new dog catcher loved him. He would put Sammy in his truck and drive him back home instead of taking him to the pound. It was in this way that Sammy lived a long and happy life, with many friends. Mary says of him, "This is Sammy's story. Maybe it's a story about what life was like in a small town, years ago, or maybe it's about the wonderful things that can happen if you break the ropes that are holding you."[20] That's the hope that Jesus brings to the world. Repentance is breaking those ropes that are holding us and moving into the hope of a better future, and we do it not to get Jesus to forgive us. We do it because Jesus *has already* forgiven us.

One of my favorite musical plays comes from a children's story that's called *Beauty and the Beast*. It's the story of a selfish prince, who was cursed by a wicked witch and turned into a beast, and the only way he could ever be changed back into a prince again is if someone chose to kiss the Beast's ugly face. That was very unlikely.

He truly was a beast. He captured an old man who became lost near his castle, and he imprisoned him in the castle. His daughter, who was

---

20 Mary Oliver, *Ropes* in *Dog Songs* (London; Penguin Books, 2015), 43.

called Beauty in the story, came to Beast and begged for her father's release. The Beast agreed only if she would remain in the place of her father. She stayed, and her father was released.

Over time, she began to feel compassion for Beast, and one day, she even kissed his ugly cheek, which changed him instantly back into a handsome prince - and the couple lived happily ever after in the castle.

The reason that's such a popular play, drawing people from around the world, is something that many of them don't even know. The reason is because it's the gospel. That is why it's popular. It's the blessing before repentance that brings about a change worthy of repentance. That's how much people hunger for the gospel. If they can't find it in church, they will find it in the theatre.

Does forgiveness always result in repentance? Sadly, the answer is no. But it's the best way that God knows to bring it about. It's the reason Jesus took it all about the countryside, and it's the reason he took it all the way to the cross. It is truly a love that will not let us go.

I heard once of a brother of a famous preacher, who was himself a preacher. When he came to his brother's church to fill in for him while he was away on vacation, he said, "My brother is a better preacher than I am, but he doesn't have a better gospel." No one has a better gospel than the one afforded to every preacher and to every church. When repentance becomes a gift instead of a burden, who would not freely embrace it?

When I was a small boy, my grandmother on my father's side lived between the school and my house, so I stopped there all the time on my way home from school. All through my elementary school days I did that. My grandfather was the librarian at the high school. He was a multi-talented man who had a small garden beside the house.

One day he said to me, "I have to be out of town for four days of continuing education, and I'd like you to weed the garden for me." I told him I would, but I got busy the next day and overlooked it. The following day, I had a lot of homework to do, and the time got away from me. On the day he was to return, I still hadn't weeded the garden.

I ran home from school to get it done, but I found him already out there, weeding the garden. He said, "You must have gotten busy this week." He forgave me. He didn't scold me. He didn't say, "Why didn't you do what you told me you'd do?" He absolved my guilt. What a terrific man he was, and what an influence on my young life! He freed me up. I was free to go and do whatever I wanted to do that afternoon.

I was also free to do what I did, pick up a hoe and join him, weeding the garden. He was just so good to me. I believe that's why people want to follow Jesus. Not because he says, "Repent and grovel here in the dirt and I will forgive you." It's because he offers us his love and acceptance up front, when we least deserve it. That's why we repent.

Ordinarily we teach our young students in this country to think big, "The world is yours for the changing. The opportunities are limitless. Don't sell yourself short. Think big. You can do big things."

It's always been interesting to me that Jesus taught just the opposite. He taught his disciples to think small. No one was too insignificant for his care. He stopped on the way to something very important to attend to the needs of people that his culture thought of as "small fries."

He taught that God loves all as God loves each, and God loves each as if they were the only one to love. That's a part of his gospel. Paul understood this very well, and he took up this theme in all of his churches. "Encourage the weak, the little ones," he taught. "Encourage the timid and the weak and the fallen ones." What a noble calling!

According to Luke, Jesus' first sermon highlighted what his ministry would be about. Hear it once more: "The Spirit of the Lord is upon me, because he has anointed me to bring good news to the poor. He has sent me to proclaim release to the captives, recovery of sight to the blind, to let the oppressed go free, and to proclaim the year of the Lord's favor."

The gospel of Jesus is good news to the poor in spirit, who realize they could never be good enough to earn God's favor. It's good news to those who are captive to their own bad choices, with the need to start over. It's good news to those who have been blind to God's love for them and now see it clearly in Jesus Christ. It's good news to those who have been oppressed with bad news for years and now want to be set free from that. It is life-changing to come to that realization.

Once when his disciples accompanied Jesus up on the mountain, they saw him transfigured before their very eyes, and it was life changing for them. It's called a theophany, a visitation from God. Their eyes were opened to something wonderful. As Elizabeth Barrett Browning has put it, "Every bush is on fire with God, but few of us see it and take off our shoes."

You just never know when God's grace will come to you in a powerful, life changing way. It can be at church, not always but sometimes. It can be in a piece of music, in a book, or a movie, but suddenly you know you are in the presence of something holy. Carlyle Marney used to say that God would surely walk to where you are and nestle in close to you, and you'd be changed by it. That's when you will realize that God is in the toughest of situations, always with you, always there to help you, to provide you with love and forgiveness, perseverance and hope.

Why is such good news difficult for some to believe? It's because we've been raised on negative talk. That even happens in church. That's how the word "preach" got a negative connotation. If someone is fussing, people often say, "Don't you preach at me!" Preaching should have a good connotation.

I remember something I heard many years ago from a pastor from Louisville, Kentucky, named Wayne Dehoney. It seems there was a man who took his bird dog out with him on a hunt. He shot a bird over a lake, and the bird fell into the lake. He sent his dog in after it, and the dog walked across the water and picked up the bird and brought it back.

The man couldn't believe his eyes. He shot another bird over the lake and sent the dog in after it. Again, the dog walked on water to get it. "Unbelievable!" the man thought, so he did it a third time, and the dog walked on water just as if it were glass. The man thought, "No one will believe this." He went back into town and got the most upstanding citizen he knew. He brought him out to the lake and said, "Watch this."

He shot another bird over the lake and sent the dog in after it, and sure enough, the dog walked on water. He did it a second time and a third. And the citizen didn't say a word.

Finally, the hunter asked, "Did you see the dog go get that bird?" "Yep." "Well, did you notice anything unusual about it?" And the man said, "Sure I did. He can't swim, can he?"

Unfortunately, that's why some people can't hear the gospel. They've heard too much negative stuff to repent and believe the good news, or to say it in our language, to change their minds.

I served two churches in cities. The other four were in small towns. There are advantages to both. But in the small towns, one of the advantages was the ecumenism that comes with a community thanksgiving service. That's when all the churches in town gather for a service, usually on the Wednesday night before Thanksgiving, to give thanks as one body.

A different church hosted the service each year, and a different preacher delivered the sermon. On one such occasion, we were hosting the service in our church, and a pastor from one of the other churches took his turn at delivering the thanksgiving sermon.

This is how it sounded: "We're just not thankful anymore. People aren't thankful. They will gather tomorrow and eat turkey and watch football, but nobody will be thankful. Nobody will be giving thanks." I remember thinking, "Well that's why we came here tonight. Why don't you just let us be thankful and stop fussing?" But he went on and on.

"Just look at these empty pews tonight. Where are all the people? They're not here, because we're not thankful anymore." I remember thinking, "No, they're not here, because they've learned we won't let them be thankful when they get here. We'll just fuss, because there aren't more people. We've turned good news into something negative." I'm not sure where all the people were that night, but wherever it was, I wish I had been with them.

How can we change that connotation of preaching after people grew up hearing negative stuff? I think the clue can be found in the gospel according to Matthew, where the Sermon on the Mount told us how

Jesus preached. It began this way: *"When Jesus saw the crowds his disciples came to him, and he opened his mouth and said, 'Blessed are you.'"* Jesus didn't come to fuss at people. He came to bless them, and only when preachers follow his example are they preaching the gospel. Some won't be able to hear it. Their ears have been damaged by the negative. But some will, and it'll be worth the effort.

On one such occasion, the disciples brought Jesus a man who couldn't speak and couldn't hear. Jesus touched his ears, and he touched his tongue, and then he said the Aramaic word that means "open up." Whatever was blocking his ears and gripping his tongue, gave way, and the man was healed. It is a moving story from the gospel of Mark, and it causes me to think: If you found yourself before Jesus, "where would you want to be touched?"

Would it be some place on your body that hurts? Would it be some deep, dark place in your heart, where you wish to be forgiven and set free from remorse? Perhaps it would be a place in your heart that is heavy with grief. Where would you wish to be touched? It is the responsibility of every church and every preacher to share the gospel each week in such a way that Jesus can touch people where they most need it.

This assignment is not just for preachers and for churches, but for every disciple who understands and has been touched by the gospel. The loving Spirit of Jesus is just as present where you are as any of the places we read about in the gospels. You are one of the fortunate ones that knows, after Jesus' resurrection, he no longer is restricted by time or by place.

He can be with us anywhere and can even go back in time to forgive those sins of yesterday that linger in our conscience. He can be with us, wherever and however we are hurting. What a treat it is to know and to be able to share the hope of that good news! The ways it can be shared are limitless.

Years ago, I saw a comedy that starred Jack Nicholson called *About Schmidt.* Schmidt was a man who retired, and his wife died shortly thereafter. On top of this, his daughter was about to marry a complete nerd, and all this causes Schmidt, at age 67, to take a hard look at his life. It wasn't a pretty picture.

His marriage had not always been a good one. His job gave him no satisfaction at all. He felt like he never really did much that mattered, and when he retired, it was not 24 hours before everything moved right on, as if he had never even worked at his company.

One day he was sitting in front of his television, when he came across the faces of hungry children, and an invitation to adopt one of them by sending $22.00 a month. He did it, and he got a little child named Ndugu.

He had bought a motor home and planned to tour the country with his wife, so he set out alone, and all along the way he was writing letters to Ndugu, reviewing his life, his failures, and his vanished dreams. It was way too mature for a boy, six years old, in Tanzania. But Schmidt wrote and sent money, sometimes extra money.

His travels were dreary, because he was lost. His life amounted to nothing. There was no meaning. When he got back home, he was sitting at his desk, feeling he had made no difference in the world whatsoever to a single human being, and he noticed he had a letter from Tanzania. It was a note from a nun at the orphanage where Ndugu lived. She was writing to say thank you to him for what his letters and support meant. She said, "I'm enclosing a painting Ndugu wants you to have." When he unfolded the paper, there were two stick figures, one adult and one child, and they were holding hands.

All through his retirement, the death of his wife, and the marriage of his daughter, Schmidt never shed a tear. He had never connected with anyone, never gave of himself to anyone. But sitting with that picture in his hand, he began to cry. He had reached out beyond himself to someone else, and for the first time in his life there was meaning, and his tears were tears of joy. The gospel of kindness and caring, sharing the very grace of God with others, brings that kind of joy.

I have spoken about John Carlton, the outstanding seminary professor. It was not just the way he *taught*. It was the way he *was* that appealed to his students. I was in his office one cold winter day, and I noticed a beautiful overcoat hanging nearby. I told John I thought it was a beautiful coat, and he replied, "Do you? I just bought that last week, and I like it better than any coat I ever owned."

Our conversation was interrupted by the arrival of a foreign exchange student, who came by to see John about an assignment. Noticing that the man wasn't wearing a coat, John said, "Aren't you cold?" The student said his country was never cold, and he didn't own a coat.

Without missing a beat, and avoiding any embarrassment to the young man, John said, "Here, see if this coat fits you. I have others. I would be pleased if you would take it." The coat was a perfect fit. The student thanked him profusely and left.

We watched him from the office window, as he walked proudly back to his dorm, turning the collar up against his neck. I didn't know what to say. I was overcome by what I had just seen happen. From what I later learned, this was not the first time John had given a coat to a student.

I invited John to come to our apartment for dinner. He accepted and said, "What time should I be there?" I said, "Oh, around six." He said, "That's good. It will give me time to run some errands in Raleigh. I have to buy a coat."

There are many ways to share the good news of God's love, and kindness is just one of them. There's hope to be felt, and there's hope to be shared. If you find grace is hard to find, even in church, you can share it, and it will flow through you and bless you on its way through. That is a certainty.

Chapter 8

Learning To Trust Grace

Fred Craddock once shared a story with a group of us about the time he was asked to be a visiting teacher of a Sunday school class at a church near his house. Their lesson was the familiar passage of the father with two sons, a prodigal and an elder brother. He decided since they were so familiar with it, a good way to teach it would be to teach it backwards. That would make its point, so he arrived and began the lesson this way: "There was a young man who took his inheritance from his father and went off to a far country and wasted everything he had. He wound up having to feed pigs."

"Finally, the boy said, 'I'm going home. My father's servants are better off than I am.' But when he got close to the house, he heard laughter and music. He asked one of the servants what was going on, and the servant told him his father was giving a party for his older brother, because he had stayed at home and done what he was supposed to do."

One of the ladies in the back of the room shouted, "That's the way it should have been told in the first place!"[21] You see, a lot of people have a problem with grace. We want to earn our acceptance, not trust God for it. We're so trained in doing the right thing and believing the right thing that we have a hard time understanding God's love for someone who didn't do the right thing and didn't believe the right thing.

But Jesus taught that God is a God of grace, and God wants to give that grace to the most undeserving of us. And if we don't see God as a God of grace, we will never see God clearly at all. That's why Jesus told Nicodemus that he needed to be born anew, from above.

It's a good analogy, because we don't earn our first birth. Our mothers do it for us out of sheer grace, and so it is with birth from above.

21 J. Lynn White, "Biblical Preaching Journal), (2005); 32.

We must let God do it for us, as sheer grace.

Of course, it's a good thing to know the Bible and to do good deeds. That pleases God, but you could never know it well enough, or do it well enough, or believe it perfectly enough, to be accepted. If you think those other things earn you acceptance, and you fail, you'll think you're not God's child anymore. That's not what made you God's child in the first place. It was God's gift.

Nicodemus came to Jesus with a cup full of good works, and Jesus taught him that you bring an empty cup to God, and God will fill it with grace. Grace upon grace comes to us like that. You never know how or when God will shed some new grace upon you, but you can appreciate it when it comes.

I went to a mentor once and said, "I feel like my faith is fading away." He said something I've never forgotten. "Jack, sometimes we have to hold on to someone else, who is holding on to God, until we get our own faith back." That was pure grace at a time of need.

On another occasion I asked him, "How can I know I have truly been called for a life in ministry?" He said, "Jack, God calls everyone, and then has to make do with those who say yes." Once again, it was another moment of grace.

All of us can be channels of grace like that. That's why Jesus called us "salt and light." It doesn't take a lot of salt to do the job, and it doesn't take a lot of light to make a difference in a dark room. We don't have to be a brilliant blaze or a powerful army. Every time you have helped someone else's children, every time you forgave someone that no one else would forgive… every time you were there for someone going through a great darkness in their lives… when you participated in giving someone who was hungry something to eat or clothes to wear… every time you sacrificed your own good for the good of someone else… you were being salt and light. You were a channel of God's grace. You made a difference in someone's life. And the more you share grace, the more you'll learn to trust it.

When I was a boy there was a television program called "The Millionaire." It was about a man who gave a gift of a million dollars, tax free, to unsuspecting people, and each episode was about how that changed those who received it. The rich donor was named John Beresford Tipton, and he had a servant named Michael Anthony, who delivered the good news to the unsuspecting recipients. I can remember thinking what a wonderful job it would be to give the gift of a million dollars on behalf of a rich donor. But what Jesus has done for us is greater than that. He has entrusted us with the gift of grace, and we can freely share it every single day of our lives.

Some people are afraid to bless other people with grace, afraid they'll be rejected, or afraid they'll fail at trying to be of help. It's a risk you have to take, but it's always worth the risk.

Frank Pollard spoke of a man who died, and in his will he left his farm to someone named Pot. They couldn't find anyone by that name, so no one broke the ground, no one sowed any seed, no one tended the fences, and nobody tended the barns. Finally, sure enough, the farm went to *pot*. And that's just the way life is. If we don't take the opportunity and the risk to bless someone with the grace of God, the opportunity is gone forever.

Some people disqualify themselves. They say, "I'm not worthy to bear God's grace. My life is filled with sins and failures." But the most helpful people in the world are those who have failed and learned from it.

I think of Simon Peter. Jesus said to him, "After you have returned, strengthen your brothers." He knew he was going to fail, but he didn't disqualify him. The same thing was true of Paul. He had persecuted Christians and even killed some of them. But look how God used him to bless the rest of us.

Never disqualify yourself. God doesn't disqualify you. God doesn't give up on anybody. Those who have received the most grace are the very ones equipped to share that grace with others. Trust the grace that has forgiven you and bless someone else by what you've learned. Look at the life of John Newton. He had been the captain of a slave ship. He kidnapped people, and many of them died on the trip across the ocean. Others were badly mistreated by their masters. That took some grace to forgive John Newton, but he didn't disqualify himself, and we're still singing *Amazing Grace*, the hymn he wrote.

In the days of Moses, when people contracted leprosy, they had to present themselves to the village priest, who was also the medical authority. He would examine the person to see if the skin condition was superficial or deep into the skin. If the infection was deep, the person was quarantined.

In order to do this, a priest had to have keen eyes. He had to not only see the infection, but also the healthy flesh around it. To be a priest you had to be able to see the festering sores of people, but also the parts that remained clean and healthy.

Nobody could do that better than Jesus. He helped those who had sinned to see themselves as human beings, not human doings. He could see the "what yet might be" in the worst of sinners, and never identified them by their worst moments. That is at the very heart of grace.

Pat Conroy wrote a wonderful book he called, "My Losing Season" in which he told of his experience of playing on the basketball team at the Citadel. When he was interviewed about the book, he told the interviewer, "I've seen winners, guys who won national championships and never got over it. They live forever in the past of their accomplishments. But a guy on a losing team never does that, because he has to pick himself up and go forward. My losing season on a basketball team has helped me in my career as a writer. I've seen writers wilt and suffer when they get bad reviews. I just think of them as a game I lost. And there's always another game tomorrow."[22]

At my last church in Knoxville, Tennessee, one of the members of the church was the former University of Tennessee athletic director, Bob Woodruff. Years before, he had served as the head football coach at Baylor University and at the University of Florida. Shortly before we

22 My Losing Season, by Pat Conroy, Bantam Books, 2003

had Bob's funeral, his son Joe shared an interesting insight about his father.

The Woodruff family was a sports family, and they knew what it was like to see Bob both worshiped and hated, depending upon wins and losses. That made his son pull for him and his teams like no one else. When Tennessee would win a big game, Joe would be ecstatic. He would go outside and replay the game on the front lawn. He would talk about it and talk about it. He would be so excited he could hardly go to sleep. But his dad would say, "Now son, there's always another game."

On the days when Tennessee lost, Joe said it was like a death in the family. He would mope around, as if his life would never be the same. But his dad would always say, "Now son, there's always another game."

Joe said, "That has kept me from being too absorbed with my successes in life, and too defeated by my failures." It's a wonderful lesson to learn, and it's absolutely necessary for a person of grace.

In one of his parables, Jesus pictured God as a great seed thrower, a seed thrower like none you've ever seen, because he throws seed everywhere. He feeds the birds, bounces it off rocks, and doesn't worry about wasting it. It was Jesus' way of saying that God shares his grace with everyone, not just a few.

The Pharisees didn't like that. They wanted God's seeds of acceptance to fall only on Jewish people, not Samaritans, not gentiles, not sinners, or those they had expelled from their synagogues. But Jesus said, 'God throws his seeds of love and acceptance on everyone, and God's love and grace is so extravagant that when one sinner comes home, God throws a party in heaven.'

In the movie *Saving Private Ryan,* there is a true story of a young man whose brothers had all been killed in the war, and President Roosevelt didn't want his mother to lose all her boys, so he sent an expedition out to find him. Tom Hanks is the actor who played the leader of that expedition.

All the men in that expedition suffered greatly to save that boy. In fact, Hanks' character gave his life to save him. As he laid dying, he looked up at Private Ryan, standing over him, and said, "Earn this." And in the final scene of the movie, Private Ryan, now a very old man, visited the grave of the man who gave his life to save him. He collapsed in tears, tormented by the idea that he had not lived a life worthy of earning such a great sacrifice.

Hear the good news. When Jesus gave his life for us on the cross he didn't say, "Earn this." No one has to earn anything. God's grace is like the seeds of the seed thrower. Do you need forgiveness? Here it comes. Do you need comfort? Here it comes. Do you need to know you are loved? Here it comes. You catch the seeds and let them grow within you, and then you become a person of grace, more forgiving, more caring, and more loving. It's a matter of learning to trust grace.

Mrs. Lake was a woman who taught the sixth grade, and she had in her class a little boy who was the son of abusive parents. Their house was a battleground.

At the end of each school year came the day for the parent-teacher conferences, and on the blackboard, Mrs. Lake had listed the hours that each parent was scheduled to come and meet with her. But this boy knew his parents wouldn't be coming. They had thrown their letter from the teacher into the trash can, and he saw that.

On the day of the conferences, parents came to the school all day long. Finally, at the end of the day, Mrs. Lake asked this little boy to remain and talk with her. She said, "First of all, I want you to know how very important you are to me. And secondly, you need to know it's not your fault that your parents didn't come here today. You deserve a conference just like all the other boys and girls, whether your parents are here or not."

She went over some of his work and explained how he ranked nationally. She wanted him to know what a wonderful student he was. When she finished, she gave him a big hug, and he went home.

That boy, today, is a grown man, and he says that conference was the turning point of his life. Mrs. Lake might not have thought she had done any earth shattering thing there that day. About all she did was to offer grace the only way she knew how. But what Jesus did with it is another story.

The grace of God is not about big things. It's about little things offered freely. "I didn't know the good news that God was a God of love and mercy. Did you tell me?" "I was all alone. Did you come to see me?" "I was imprisoned by my own bad health. Did you visit me?" "I was hungry in a world of plenty. Did you offer me anything?" "I was without good clothing. I waited for the styles to change, hoping you would give me some of your old clothes. Did you offer me anything?" "I was a stranger, new in the community. I didn't know a single soul. Did you introduce yourself to me?"

Jesus knows our resources for grace are far more than we may think. It's a matter of learning to trust the grace we've been given to eventually bless others as well. Trusting grace is a lot like being a leaf on one of God's trees. They endure heat and cold, wind and rain, drought and even hail. Their lives are not easy but they hang on in trust, and at the time of their death, they just turn loose and throw themselves into the wind of God's spirit.

Tom Long described a saint as someone whose life manages to be a cranny through which the infinite peeps. We allow a little bit of God's kindness, generosity, and mercy to peep through, and every time we do that, someone gets a glimpse of God's grace.

John Claypool defined the gospel of Jesus in five stanzas. "You are forgiven. You are loved. You are wanted. You are needed. Come home." The good news is you are a saint. You are a carrier of that gospel.

Grace is kind to those who experience little kindness, forgiving to those who experience little forgiveness, loving to those experiencing hate, and caring to those, who are experiencing loneliness and pain. The final word of God is always mercy.

Did you ever hear the true story of the day there was a total eclipse in colonial New England? It was back in the day when eclipses still horrified people with the threat of doom. They thought it was the end of the world. Some still do. It becomes pitch dark in the middle of the day.

Several of the legislators moved for adjournment, so they could be with their families for the end. But one of them said, "Mr. Speaker, if it's not the end of the world and we adjourn, we're going to look like fools. And even if it is the end of the world, I should choose to be found doing my duty. I make a motion, sir, that candles be brought."

There are dark moments in everyone's life. This life can be downright mean. But those with the grace of God have the candle, and the candle shines in the darkness and the darkness has never overcome it. That candle is grace.

It reminds the world that God's goodness is bigger than all our badness, God's love is stronger than the entire world's hate, and God's mercy is greater than all our sin. It's a kindly light we have been given. The responsibility of every preacher, of every church, and of every Christian is to let it shine. It is scarce in today's world.

Luke explained the grace of God in an incredible way. He said God is kind to the ungrateful and the wicked. Jesus believed that those of us created in the image of God have it within us to behave like God, with kindness and mercy. Yet, one prominent scholar said he no longer goes to church because he can't find any grace there.

He's not the only one. Churches everywhere are decreasing in attendance. It's happening across the nation. There are all kinds of theories, as to why this is happening.

William McKinney says it's due to the declining birthrates in this country. Tony Campolo has said it is America's affluence. Martin Marty said it is the weekend trips people take today. John Buchanan said it's the lack of outreach on the part of churches. Will Willimon said it's the time of our services — eleven o'clock on Sunday morning. He says not even the Rotary Club would meet at such a time.

It could be a little of all of that, but I agree with the one who said it is the lack of mercy and grace that people find in church. I believe people want to find Jesus there, the one who was kind to the ungrateful and wicked. They're looking for a small group, whose ways are not the world's ways and whose thoughts are not the world's thoughts.

They don't need entertainment. They get that at a dozen places all week long. They don't need judgment and guilt. They have so much of that now that they can't carry it. Whether they even know it or not, they're looking for grace.

Thank God for those saints who let a glimmer of grace shine through. How refreshing they are! Remember the story of Jacob and Esau? Jacob had stolen his brother's inheritance, and Esau had pledged to kill him when he saw him again. Twenty years later, they met face to face, and Esau didn't condemn him or try to harm him. Instead, he reached out and hugged him and wept tears of reconciliation.

Jacob was so relieved and so inspired by that, he said to his brother, "Seeing your face is like seeing the face of God." Esau's grace reminded Jacob of the grace of God. See how it works? Have you ever experienced anything like that? Have you ever been up against it, and someone's friendly face represented for you the very face of God? Have you told them? You should do that. Paul experienced it multiple times.

When he was blinded, bewildered, and so frightened he couldn't eat or drink, the very man he had gone to Damascus to persecute came to him, put his arms around him, and said, "Brother Saul. The Lord sent me so that you could see again." I'm sure when Paul saw Ananias, it was like the face of God.

Later, when Paul went to Jerusalem to tell the apostles the story of his experience with God, nobody believed him. They didn't trust him. That's when a man named Barnabas put his arm around him and vouched for him. I'm sure that face looked like the face of God to Paul.

When he was in prison, all alone and cold, and the Philippian church sent a man named Epaphroditus to bring him their love, as he looked through the bars and saw that friendly face, it must have looked like the face of God.

Have you ever been a face like that for someone? Roger Lovette use to tell the story of Herbert Oliver, a black civil rights preacher who grew up in Alabama. He was raised in poverty, when his folks were paid less than white folks for the same day's work. They had no civil rights. They had inferior schools and used textbooks that were worn out and cast off by white schools.

One day, when they had little to eat, his mother gave him a quarter and told him to go to the store to buy a can of syrup. That evening she was going to serve her children syrup and biscuits for supper. It was all she could afford. Little Herbert got the syrup and started back home, swinging the bucket, and the handle came off.

The can went sailing through the air and landed so hard it broke open, and all the syrup spilled out on the ground. Herbert began to cry. He tried to put the syrup back in the can with his hands, but that didn't work very well. Just as he was getting it all over himself, a man walked up behind him and said, "Son, I don't believe that's going to work. Wipe your hands off in the grass, and let's go back to the store."

They went back to the store, and the man bought him another can of syrup and sent him on his way. Dr. Oliver later wrote of that experience and said, "I'd never met the man. I don't even know who he was. But he looked like God."[23] That's what happens when grace is shared. And just think, before the week is over, someone could say that about you.

---

23 Sermon delivered at Baptist Church of the Covenant, Birmingham, Alabama by Roger Lovette.

Chapter 9

Recognizing Grace

A Roman Catholic priest by the name of William Bausch told of attending a huge semi-Gothic cathedral when he was just a little boy. At the highest part of the large sanctuary was a single enormous eye, like you find on the back of a dollar bill, and that eye just about scared little William to death.

One day, he went into the sanctuary after school for children's choir practice, but he arrived early, and the only other person in that vast sanctuary was an older lady, saying her prayers and lighting candles. She noticed him sitting across the way, staring at that eye.

She knew the symbolic meaning of the eye. It comes from Psalm 121, *"The God who watches over Israel neither slumbers or sleeps."* It was meant to comfort but he was scared to death, so she went over to where he was seated and said, "That eye scares you, doesn't it?" He nodded yes. She said, "You think that's God watching you to see if you do something wrong, so he can punish you, don't you?" He nodded yes.

She had seen this happen to her own children years before, so she said, "That's not what it means, honey. Has anyone ever told you what that eye means?" He shook his head no.

She knew he probably wouldn't understand the Psalm 121 explanation, so she summed it up as beautifully as anyone could do for a small child. She said, "It means every time you come into this room and see that eye, you can remember that God loves you so much he can't take his eyes off of you." Father Bausch says, "After that day, every time I came in the church and saw that eye, I would wave and say, "Hello God, it's me, Billy. And I love you too." That boy grew up to be a priest.[24]

24   William Bausch, "A World of Stories for Preachers and Teachers" (Mystic, CT: Twenty-Third Publications, 1998).

Grace is a beautiful thing to recognize. There's a story in 2 Kings (6:8-23) about the prophet Elisha that illustrates it well. One morning, Elisha's young servant rushed inside in a panic. He said, "In the night, the enemy has encircled us. I went outside this morning, and in every direction all I can see are Syrians, and the Syrians hate us. We are under siege. Our lives are gravely threatened."

Instead of responding in panic like his servant, the prophet simply fell to his knees and said, "O God, open the eyes of this young man. Help him to see that those that are with us are greater than those that are with them." Something happened to the eyes of the young man, as the prophet prayed. He looked back outside and could see beyond the Syrians that there were angelic hosts of greater number and potency than the enemy possessed.

John told us in his gospel that we have been given grace upon grace. There are physical eyes and spiritual eyes, and it takes spiritual eyes to recognize the grace all around you.

Something like that happened at the crucifixion of Jesus. As Jesus was dying, the most hardened person, the man who had presided over many crucifixions, suddenly had his eyes opened to grace and praised God saying, "Surely this man was the Son of God." Christian tradition says he resigned his job, became a believer, and lived as one of the great Christians of the first century. We can see how that tradition began. It was because of the opening of spiritual eyes to the grace of God.

The *Ars Moriendi* is a body of Christian literature that originally provided guidance for those who were dying back in the fifteenth century. It pictures a dying person all by himself or herself when Satan comes to them. Here is how it reads:

Satan: You are frightened, aren't you?

Dying Person: Yes, I am frightened, but I'm trusting in my Savior, who calms all my fears.

Satan: Oh really? You think you're going to be rewarded by this Jesus, don't you? You, who have no righteousness?

Dying Person: Christ is my righteousness.

Satan: Oh, Christ is your righteousness? You think Christ is going to bring you into the company of Peter and Paul? You, who have sinned so badly, over and over?

Dying Person: No, I'm not going into the company of Peter and Paul. I'm going into the company of the thief on the cross.

Satan: Why are you so confident? You, who have done nothing good?

Dying Person: I have a good God, who judges with mercy.

Satan: Legions of demons are salivating, waiting for your soul.

Dying Person: I would be hopeless and fearful of that if the Lord had not already crushed your tyranny.

Satan: Your God is unjust. What kind of God would bring someone like you into a kingdom of righteousness?

Dying Person: He keeps his promises and that is what justice is, and I will call on his mercy.[25]

A devotional literature, originally written to erase the fears of the dying, became a literature that was also read by the living, as the writers attempted to open the eyes of their readers to the grace that is their hope. William Langdon wrote something 600 years ago that described that grace as well as it can be described. He wrote, "All the wickedness of the world, which people may do or think, is no more to the mercy of God than a live coal dropped in the sea."

Up in New England during certain seasons of the year, you can walk along the beach and notice boats high and dry up on the beach, a long way from the water. Those who are not familiar with the ocean may ask, "How will they ever get those boats back down in the water?" But those familiar with the ocean will tell you that if you wait long enough, the ocean will come to the boat. In the fullness of time, the tide comes in. That's how it is with God's grace. It comes when it's really needed, if we have the eyes to see it.

---

25 Ars Moriendi in Nancy Lee Beaty, *The Craft of Dying* (London, Yale University Press, 1970).

On a personal level, I can remember one such night as I traveled home from a preaching assignment in another city. I was tired and weary, and my faith was about as weak as a tea bag that had been used a hundred times. I felt alone, as one who had lost his way.

But I had in the car with me some tapes John Claypool had sent me, and I was listening to them as I drove home. One of the lectures John was delivering affected me unlike anything I had ever experienced in my entire life. I had heard sermons and lectures by the hundreds for fifty years. I'd been a Christian for a long time, and a preacher for longer than I could remember. But nothing like this had ever happened to me before.

The message of the gospel became so vividly apparent that it was as if a mighty wind had passed over me. I was deeply, deeply affected. I got my faith back and realized like no other time that I was loved. The tears streamed down my face as I listened to John. It felt as if the Good Shepherd himself had found me and brought me back home, because he had. I understood the phrase "surprised by joy" that night.

Years ago, someone told me about a boy named Brenning, who felt he wanted to be a minister but people discouraged him because he was so short and didn't have a good speaking voice. After two years in college, Brenning was about to change his mind, but he met two men who helped him to avert that.

One of the men was named Slaughter, who counseled Brenning to be himself and to not listen to all the naysayers. He told him, "Do what's in your heart." The other man was named Hortzwaller, an older pastor. Brenning went with him one day to a funeral. When they arrived at the cemetery, all the people were leaving. They had gone to the wrong grave! Old Hortzwaller simply said, "Oh well, I'll do better tomorrow," and they finally found the right grave.

Brenning said he learned to do what was in his heart from Slaughter, and he learned not to take himself too seriously from Hortzwaller. He said, "God was with me in those men." He finished college and went on to get a Ph.D. from Vanderbilt. He became one of the greatest preachers and teacher of preachers this country has ever known, except he was known by his first name by then, the name Fred. Fred Craddock recognized God's grace in two other preachers, and just look at what it made him.[26]

I remember a friend, when I served the wonderful church in Middlesboro, Kentucky. His name was Doug Beaty. He was elected deacon while I was there and given a list of families to be under his special care. I visited with one of those members one day and she said, "I want you to look at this." She took me to the kitchen and showed me a pan of homemade rolls. I said, "Those sure do look good. Did you make them?" She said, "No. Doug Beaty brought them to me. He's my deacon. He put the sweetest note inside. It said, 'I hope these rolls make your day brighter.'"

I mentioned that to another person that I visited, and he said, "I'm in his deacon family too. He brought me some of those rolls when I was sick, and the note said, "I hope you're feeling better." Later, another person told me, "I got some too, just last week, and my note said, "God loves you and is with you."

I spoke with Doug about those rolls he had learned to bake. I said, "I'm finding people who sure are enjoying the rolls you're taking them." He said, "Well, I wanted to do something to express care, so I decided to learn to make homemade rolls."

People make rolls all the time. I am aware of that. But when Jesus breathes on the baker, and the Holy Spirit gets a hold of those rolls, and someone, in a moment of difficulty or struggle, is suddenly made aware of God's grace in their time of need, those rolls become more than just rolls. People recognized grace that surprised them with joy because of Doug Beaty.

Norman Cousins told about going to Africa to visit Albert Schweitzer, the great missionary. Schweitzer had left a career as a doctor and theologian to become a missionary. He'd also left the ability to fill any

---

26 Gary Carver, *A Slave to Mistaken Notions, Sermons for Advent, Christmas, and Epiphany* (Lima, Ohio: CSS Publishing, 2003), 214.

great concert hall, because he was such a wonderful organist, one of the finest interpreters of Bach of his day. But he left it all to go to Africa.

When Cousins visited him, he said that every evening. after dinner, Schweitzer would follow the same practice. He would fold his napkin, walk over to the upright piano, and play a hymn. Earlier that evening Cousins had noticed that piano was at least fifty years old, its keyboard badly stained. Every ivory key was held down with large double screws. It was in awful shape.

On that evening, Schweitzer sat down at the bench, and propped open his hymnbook, and played that awful piano. Cousins said it lost its poverty in his hands. Its capacity for music was fully realized.[27]

That is exactly how God's grace is recognized. By some great miracle, God takes the efforts of everyday people and makes out of it something beautiful to behold. John Claypool could have never known what he was doing at that moment for me, alone in my car. Those two preachers could never have known that they were encouraging one who would become one of America's greatest preachers. Doug Beaty could have never known the grace people would find in a pan of rolls. Grace always surprises us with joy, when our eyes are opened.

John Killinger has said that Jesus was God's way of getting rid of a bad reputation. What he meant by that, of course, was that when people could see God in a form they could understand, their picture of God changed from the primitive understanding that they had back in Old Testament days. He said the Baptist church in which he grew up, however, was sadly unaware of the picture of God that Jesus painted.

He said the God portrayed in that church was jealous in the worst sense of that word, was demanding, inflicting, peevish, punitive, and resentful, all the things that love is not. They understood God to be powerful, but mean and vengeful, never willing to forget anyone's sins. Even if God was said to forgive their sins through the blood of Jesus, there was always the implication that they were written down in a great book somewhere and would be brought out at the most embarrassing

27 Norman Cousins, *Albert Schweitzer's Mission* (London: Penguin Books, 1985),

moment.[28]

Killinger said he knew that wasn't right, even when he was a child. How on earth did he know that? Who taught him? It obviously wasn't anyone in his church. The wind of the Holy Spirit blew, and young John was listening and recognized grace. That wind blows as it will.

I understood Killinger's words the minute I heard them. I remember hearing great preachers tell me of God's grace and love in ways I had never heard before, and I told others, "I have believed what he said all my life, but I'm surprised to finally hear a preacher say it." We recognize grace when we hear it. That is the work of God's own spirit.

Someone told me the story of a timid orphan, who was terrified by a fire and brimstone preacher. She went home to visit her own pastor and broke down in tears. He said to her, "What's the matter, my dear?" She told him she had been to hear Reverend Brown preach, and she hadn't been able to live with herself since, because she just knows she is one of the wicked ones that God hates, and she knew she would never get to heaven because she forgot God sometimes. Reverend Brown had said that the wicked and all nations that forget God will be turned into hell, and the little girl said, "I just can't stand it."

Her pastor looked in her eyes and said, "Do you sometimes forget your own daddy, Annie?" He had died a few years before. Annie said, "I remember him most days, but sometimes I forget." "Do you think your daddy would be angry with his child because she was so busy with her books or play that she didn't think of him every day?" "No sir, I don't. He wouldn't be angry with me for that. He would probably say, 'She will think about me another day. There's time enough.' That's what he would say."

"Well then, Annie," said the wise pastor, "do you not think your heavenly father is as kind as your earthly father?" "I hadn't thought of it like that," said Annie. And the pastor said, "Apparently, neither did Reverend Brown, Annie."

28 John Killinger, T*en Things I Learned Wrong From a Conservative Church*(New York: Crossroad Publishing Company, 2002), 41.

That little girl had been scared to death by someone's preaching, even though the Bible clearly says perfect love casts out fear. She had been scared, of all people, by a preacher of the gospel. But she recognized grace when she heard it in the voice of her own pastor. Grace isn't grace at all until it is recognized. But by the love of grace itself, we are given the ability to recognize it when we hear it or see it. Otherwise, our lives would be total chaos and fear.

God's grace empowers us and helps us up when we've fallen. It never beats us down, and it never allows us to disqualify ourselves from future service. That's what is so sad about the story of Judas. He thought he was too broken to mend. God's grace would have forgiven him and repaired him, but he disqualified himself.

Jesus once told a story about a boy who tried to disqualify himself. He had left his father and recklessly used up his father's resources. When he realized how lost he had become, he decided to return to his father, but when he got home he just wanted a servant's job. He didn't see himself as being worthy of being in the family. He tried to disqualify himself, but his father said, "My son is back." Grace doesn't disqualify us and doesn't allow us to disqualify ourselves either, and that boy recognized that, when his father threw a celebration in his honor. "My son was lost, but now he is found."

Peter speaks of recognizing what grace can do (1 Peter 1:3-9). He had tried to disqualify himself as well, and he had gone back to his original vocation of fishing. But that's when he was surprised by joy. Jesus found him beside the sea, recognized him as lost, and found him. Peter later writes that the grace of God allows us to inherit four things: Boundless mercy. Hope for the future. The security that God never changes God's mind about us and never gives up on anyone. And finally, we inherit the last gift, joy. The first three gifts would surely produce the fourth one. Joy is always the result of recognized grace.

If those are the free gifts that God's grace permits us all to inherit, don't you find it strange that a man once asked Jesus, "What must I do to inherit eternal life?" What must I do? You don't do anything to inherit. It is done for you by the donor. But you are changed by your inheritance, and in the case of grace, you become a person of mercy. It's not something you do to be accepted. It's something you do *because* you are accepted. Once you have recognized the grace of God in your life, others will recognize that grace in you.

While I served a church in Charlotte, I also served on a council called "Charlotteans for Alternatives to the Death Penalty." It was an organization made up of clergy, lawyers, and other interested individuals. It was started by Isabel Day, the public defender, who was a member of my church, and it was formed at the time that the state of North Carolina was within months of executing the first woman in the United States in twenty years, and the first *person* in North Carolina in thirty years. The woman had been convicted of poisoning her husband, and she had spent many years in prison.

During that time, she had become a model prisoner and was used by prison authorities to counsel and influence difficult prisoners that had been admitted to the system. She was now a grandmother and they listened to her. As the time for her execution drew near, our group began to consider if there was a better way to deal with prisoners of her kind, that had been rehabilitated to a large degree and were now useful to the state.

We fashioned a bill whereby someone could receive a life sentence without parole, a law that had not yet been adopted in North Carolina. None of us who were clergy, believed that Jesus would ever find someone so hopeless that he would put them to death. To imagine Jesus killing anyone, *scheduling* their death and then carrying it out, was simply beyond belief. Yet, when we began to make the news about our suggested bill, there was heated opposition.

Personally, I was interviewed on a couple of radio programs and appeared on WBTV to explain our position and our suggestion to the legislature. The day I was to appear as a guest at the TV station, another preacher was asked to accompany me, to debate the position.

Very quickly he began to quote from Old Testament passages and from Paul's Roman letter to support the right to execute someone. I asked him to go all the way back to the very first murder in Genesis, where Cain killed his brother Abel but God didn't execute him. In fact, he said, "If anyone touches him, he will answer to me for it." But Cain had to roam the countryside without a home, because God knew people would not be as forgiving as God.

After the program I said to him, "Jesus came to reveal God to us. You are a *preacher,* for goodness sake. You have been ordained to preach the gospel and draw attention to what *Jesus* would do." But he just continued to serve up examples of killings done by Israel and the Romans in the Bible, as evidence that it was okay for us to kill people in North Carolina. In fact, both Jesus and Paul, the writer of Romans, were executed, and this fellow didn't see the irony of that.

It appeared to me then, and it appears to me now, that the church can get off track if it suits their personal prejudice or political position. We can easily forget our grace and condemn someone else. We can disqualify people that Jesus would never disqualify. We can be Christians and forget all about Jesus and what he would do and have us to do. The church was begun to do just the opposite, to be a place where God's grace would be so abundant that people would be able to recognize it everywhere.

I remember hearing of a man who grew up in a little country house that had a well out back with some of the sweetest water in the world. But progress brought plumbing to the house, so they closed the old well. That man grew up and moved away, but he kept remembering the time in his life when the water tasted so good, so he went back one day and found the well out behind the old home place, still boarded up. He uncovered it and sent a bucket down, but it was dry. He couldn't understand. It had never been dry.

He asked a neighbor about it, and the neighbor said, "That well is fed with underground springs. As long as you pump the water out and use it, it will continue. But when you stop, the water dries up." The reason people come to a church, any church, is to stand again in the springs of God's grace. What will they find?

Chapter 10

The Results Of Grace

One of the most beautiful aspects of grace in the human heart is the ability to recognize the voice of God among all the other voices that we hear daily. That is because we hear many voices that are *not* the voice of God.

Someone wants to go next door and give their neighbor a piece of their mind. They know it's not the right thing to do, so they often preface their remarks with, "God told me to come over here and tell you this." They're blaming their bad behavior on God.

Some are asked to do something in their church, such as teach a class, or serve in some position of leadership, or work with the youth, and they say, "Let me pray about it." Later they say, "No, God told me not to do it. Sorry." How can you argue with that? Of course, I've never really heard of God telling anybody not to serve.

How do we recognize God's true voice? Some preachers, mad as a boiled owl, will get up in their pulpits and skin everybody alive and say, "This is the word of the Lord." Well no, I'm afraid not. That's the word of an angry person who needed to cool off before he got up to speak.

How do you know the difference? Jesus said, "My sheep will know my voice." It's a voice that doesn't put anyone down, is a very forgiving voice, and a voice that knows the "might have been" and the "what yet may be" in people. Anytime you hear someone speaking in an ugly, accusatory, or judgmental way, it is not the voice of God. It's a human voice. Grace teaches you that.

People flocked to hear Jesus. They didn't do that for any of the Pharisees. What was the difference? They were attracted to a voice that was winsome and kind, forgiving and not condemning. Little children loved the voice of Jesus. They knew he wouldn't do or say anything to scare them. Gentiles came to hear Jesus. They knew he wouldn't reject them like other Jewish leaders.

For Jesus, religion was filled with hope. The last word was never judgment. It was always grace and mercy. God's judgment is written into the nature of the world. Never do any of us do wrong without feeling judged by our actions. However, the grace of God says, "You were wrong, but I can clean that up for you if you want me to."

The result of grace in someone's life is to make them more loving, more sensitive and kind. All the great sacrifices that people have made down through history are examples of this. Martin Luther King didn't go to Memphis because he wanted to be killed. He went because he loved the poor sanitation workers. Ministers don't take controversial stands with groups who are hated because they want to be hated also, but because they love those who are being mistreated. Why did Jesus go to Jerusalem knowing that the authorities wanted to kill him there? It was the result of grace in his life, and the love it produced for you and me.

I love the words of Robert Kennedy: "Each time a person stands up for an idea, or acts to improve the lot of others, or strikes out against injustice, that person sends out a tiny ripple of hope. And crossing each other from a million different centers of energy those ripples build a current that can sweep down the mightiest walls of oppression and resistance. Few are willing to brave the disapproval of their fellow man, the censure of their colleagues, or the wrath of their society. Yet it is essential for those who seek to change a world that yields painfully to change."[29]

Only the result of grace in a person's heart makes that possible. Who would want to tell a racist that God loves everyone? Who would tell a nation in favor of capital punishment that God doesn't want to kill even guilty people? Who would tell religious people that God is love, not wrath? Who would stand up to news organizations and tell

29 Robert Kennedy, "Ripple of Hope Speech," June 6, 1966, University of Cape Town, South Africa.

them that exposing people's moral failures is not news? Who would tell the government that God doesn't want us to settle everything with our bombs? Only someone who has been exposed to the grace of God in Jesus Christ would say any of those things. But it's the result of grace that makes it happen, that makes people want to do the loving thing and not the hateful and judgmental thing.

Will Willimon was asked to speak to a fraternity at Duke. When he arrived, he noticed a little boy there, about nine or ten years old, and when Will began to speak, the little boy fell asleep in the lap of one of the college boys. When he finished his talk, he heard the college boy say to the kid, "You go on and get ready for bed. I'll be there to tuck you in and read you a story in a minute."

Will asked that young man as he was leaving, "Who was that little boy asleep in your lap?" He answered, "Oh, that's Darrell. Our fraternity is part of the Durham Big Brother program. We met Darrell that way. His mom is on crack cocaine and having a tough time. Sometimes it gets so bad that she can't care for him, so we told Darrell to call us when he needs us, and we go over, pick him up, and let him stay with us until it's okay for him to go home. We take him to school, buy his clothes, and books and stuff."

Will said, "That's amazing." And the young man said, "Ah, we do it because we love him, I guess. What's amazing is that God could pick guys like us to do something worthwhile for someone else!"[30] That is the work of grace.

Fred Craddock used to love to talk about the time when he was a boy on a west Tennessee farm. Once, when his father was on a tractor, a lightning bolt struck the cultivator and knocked his father onto the ground. He was unconscious for four days, and they didn't know if he would survive. They lived so far away from any town or doctor that they just brought him into the house, put him in the front bedroom and watched over him all those days.

Late on one of those evenings, a man came to the house. He went in

30 Sermon preached by Nicholas Lang, St Paul's on the Green, Norwalk, CT. January 25, 2015.

the back door and into the bedroom where Fred's dad was unconscious and closed the door behind him. Fred didn't see him again until he had breakfast with them the next morning. When he finally left, Fred asked his mother, "Who was that man? Was he a doctor?" She said, "No, son, he's a minister." It was the first minister Fred ever saw in his life, but he says he wanted to be a minister ever since that day.[31] That's the result of grace. There are so very many examples of it. People are changed. They receive grace. They are grateful. And they become gracious.

Elie Wiesel suffered the Nazi concentration camps and survived. In an interview with Bill Moyers, he said he believed it was an accident that he survived while his parents and other family members did not. He didn't believe God saved him and allowed them to be killed.

Moyers asked, "Well, is life just a lottery?" Wiesel said, "Yes, there is a great randomness in this life, and there in the camps it was very much a lottery who would make it and who would not. But now that I have survived, I have to give meaning to that survival. Because I survived by accident, my survival should not remain an accident. I have to give it meaning. I have to make it stand for something. I believe that every moment is a moment of grace, and we must take advantage of it and use it gratefully."[32]

Yet another result of grace in the hearts of people is ecumenism, the cooperation within all the rooms of the house of faith. Did you know that botanists have made an interesting discovery that, when the roots of trees touch, there is a substance present that reduces growth competition? It's a fungus that helps to link the roots of all those different species of trees. A whole forest is incorporated together in this manner. One tree may have better access to nutrients, another to water, and a third to sunlight. But the trees together have the means to cooperate with one another. Grace produces that kind of cooperation among fellow Christians and churches.

They are like the man who took great pride in his lawn, but found he

---

31   Fred Craddock, Lecture at Mynatt Ministers Retreat, Gatlinburg, Tennessee.
32 Facing Hate with Elie Wiesel, interview by Bill Moyers, December 10, 2013.

was growing mainly wild violets and dandelions, to his displeasure. He tried everything to get rid of them. Still they were there at the end of the day. Finally, he wrote the US Department of Agriculture. He told them all the things he had tried to get rid of his weeds and asked of them, "What should I do now?" After a while, he got his reply. "We suggest you learn to love them."

That is what happens to people who have experienced the grace of God. They are surprised by their ability to love others who don't look like them or think like them. The secret to that is illustrated by a monastery that had fallen on bad times.

People seldom came to visit. But on the edge of the monastery was a little cabin, where an old Jewish rabbi lived. He would visit the monastery from time to time to pray. He was known as a very wise teacher. One day, the head monk visited with the wise old rabbi. The rabbi said, "I know you have come to me for a teaching. You are concerned that your monastery is not what it used to be, the monks are not close to one another anymore, and people don't visit. It isn't a place that draws others to it."

"I am going to give you one teaching that will help you, but you can repeat the teaching only once. After that you must never say it aloud again." The monk said, "Teach me." The rabbi leaned forward and whispered, "The Messiah is among you." Everything became stone silent. The rabbi said, "Now you must go." The monk left without saying a word.

The next morning, he called all the monks together and told them he had a teaching from the rabbi that could be repeated only once. Then he looked at them and said, "The rabbi said that one of us is the Messiah." The monks were startled at this teaching. What could it mean? They were deeply puzzled but did not mention it again, as they were instructed.

As time went by, the monks began to treat one another with a reverence like never before. There was genuine caring about them now. Guests who had visited were moved by the way these monks treated each other. People began to come in greater numbers, because they were moved by these men, who treated each other as though they were Christ.[33] But isn't that the secret to loving others? To treat them as though they were Jesus? That happens when people are graced with proper teaching. They have learned that it is in loving, not in being loved, that life has its greatest meaning. That's a hard lesson to learn. Only the grace of God can do that.

There was a story on NPR years ago of a reporter covering a conflict somewhere in the world. He saw a little girl who had been shot, stopped what he was doing, and rushed to a man who had picked up the little girl. He got them in his car and raced to the hospital as fast as he could.

The man said, "Please hurry, my child is still breathing." A bit later he said, "Hurry please, my child is still warm." Finally, he said, "Hurry, O God, my child is getting cold." By the time they arrived, the little girl was dead. As they washed the blood off their hands the man said, "Thank you for trying, but now I have the duty of telling the child's father that his child didn't make it and he will be heartbroken."

The reporter said, "I thought she was *your* child." And the man said, "They are *all* our children." That's the work of grace. It's a beautiful thing to have the eyes to see and the ears to hear the results of the grace of God in your life. It is a redeeming, sustaining, life changing grace. It may come when we least expect it, in ways we would never have dreamed. The ability to see and hear it come from a life steeped in grace.

Still another one of the qualities that is the unique result of grace is the ability to avoid judgmentalism. Judgment is a part of our way of life. Only those immersed in grace can begin to understand the command to "judge not," because we see it in every area of our culture. It's in our courtrooms, our churches, our schools, even in our media. We are inundated with judgment.

I remember a professor that I respected very much in seminary saying, "God didn't send his son into the world to condemn it, and it's for sure none of you were sent for that purpose either." Every time they

33 Megan Mckenna, "The Messiah is One of Us" in *Mary: Shadow of Grace* (New York: Orbis Books, 1995).

brought a sinner to Jesus, he preferred the sinners to their accusers. Every time. He never condemned sinners. He offered them forgiveness and a new start, free of the old baggage. The only harsh words Jesus ever uses in the gospels were offered, not to people who had sinned and felt ashamed, but to the self-righteous people who judged them. God's kingdom is a kingdom of mercy, and God's judgment is tempered by that mercy. His commandment to the rest of us was: "Don't try judging. You have neither the knowledge nor the virtue for the task."

You may have heard of the talent scout, who came to town in search of some talent. One man came to him and said, "I can imitate birds." The talent scout said, "Bird imitators are a dime a dozen, son. I can't use you." So, disappointed, the young man shrugged his shoulders, flapped his arms, and flew out the window." The talent scout was not a good judge.

The prophet Zechariah said you and I can't measure anything that has God in it. That included everything that God ever made, every person. Remember Mary Magdalene? If you ask most people what she was when Jesus met her, they will tell you she was a prostitute. But nowhere in the gospels does it say that. They got that from *Jesus Christ Superstar*.

The gospels said she had seven demons. Seven was a complete number in the numerology of Jesus' day. Demons meant you were physically or mentally ill. They had no knowledge of bacteria, viruses, or mental illness. They blamed all illness on demons.

Seven demons meant Mary was very sick. We don't know what it was. We only know Jesus ministered to her. But all these years later, Christian gossip says this woman was a prostitute. So much for our judgment.

The woman at the well is another example. Jesus said to her, "You have had five husbands, and the man you're with now is not your husband." Many have condemned her as an evil person for this. But Jesus wasn't condemning her. Instead, he was touching her wound and offering her healing love, because in those days a woman couldn't divorce her husband but a husband could get rid of his wife for the simplest of reasons. If she'd had five husbands, it meant five different men had abandoned her. Maybe she burned the biscuits. Maybe she became unattractive to him. Maybe she snored at night. Men could divorce a woman for any reason they chose by just handing her a piece of paper.

There was no alimony, no welfare, no work available for women, and no going back home, because a father was disgraced if a man divorced his daughter. There was nothing a woman could do to stay alive but sell her body on the street. This woman had tried to avoid that five times, and the man she was with at present wouldn't marry her.

Jesus cared about this woman. He understood what she'd been through. He knew her story, and his understanding acceptance gave her worth and dignity and the love and blessing of God. It's no wonder she went back home elated. Yet look what we've done to her. Do you see how incredibly incapable of accurately judging we can be?

I think of the story of the ten lepers that Jesus healed, and only one returned to say thank you. Jesus asked, "Where are the other nine?" Every sermon I've ever heard on this text has judged these nine men for not being grateful. But Jesus didn't judge them. He simply asked where they were. He was concerned for them because he knew the possible reasons they didn't return.

Perhaps some didn't return because they were dumbfounded by Jesus' power and were afraid of him. That happened to Jesus many times. Even his own disciples were afraid of him when they saw him calm a storm at sea. This had to disappoint him, because he didn't want anybody to be afraid of him. He came to cast out fear.

In that day, they believed that all illness was a punishment from God. Perhaps some of these nine were afraid Jesus would change his mind and punish them again if they returned.

Maybe some of these men had been taught, "Don't ever accept any handouts. Always earn your keep." But they couldn't earn the gift Jesus had bestowed upon them, so they might have been ashamed and embarrassed by that.

Or, it could be they had lived so long in degrading dependency that they forgot how to say thank you, forgot how to be grateful. Every day of their lives they'd been begging. They were not only embarrassed by the handouts, but you forget to be grateful when you spend your life saying, "Mister, can you give me a penny? Just a penny? Pennies add up. I can get bread for enough pennies. Can you spare just a penny? Don't come to close to me. I'm unclean. Just throw it over here and I'll get it." Do you have any idea what that can do to a person? It would take away all your self-respect and make you incapable of gratitude.

Maybe one or more of these lepers had a sick or dying relative at home. All those years they've been separated from him, but when they returned they found him sick and couldn't leave him. That could have been it.

Or maybe they had been through this before with some false messiah, and they thought they were healed but found out later they were still lepers. Maybe they were waiting to see if they really were healed. Those former healers could have made skeptics out of them. That could be it.

Or maybe, and this is the most likely of all, maybe when these men went to the priest to be declared clean, he asked them, "Who did this?" They said, "Jesus." And the priest said, "Do you know what a troublemaker he is? He's in all kinds of trouble with the chief priest and the authorities. You better not breathe a word of this to anybody, and don't go back there if you don't want to get in trouble too." That may be why they didn't return.

Jesus was concerned for these nine men, because he knew all those things were possibilities. He had experienced them before, when he had healed people. You and I really are bad at judging. We're not at all good at it. Jesus told us to "judge not," *not because we shouldn't, but because we can't!* But we can love and share grace. We can do that.

Craddock used a parable to illustrate this in a teaching on parables that he shared with a group of us. It goes like this: A certain man had a custom each year to send a gift of money to his poor neighbor. Again, on this year, he sent his son with the gift. But the boy returned upset and put the money back on the table. The father said, "What's wrong?" The boy said, "I was going to give him the gift like you told me, father, but when I went inside his house, I saw a very expensive bottle of wine on his table, so I just brought your money back home."

His father said, "Expensive bottle, was it? That poor man must have once been accustomed to some real good things. I'm going to double my gift to him this year. Here, take it to him."

When Fred shared that parable with us he asked, "Which of those two men do you wish to become? The son, who judged wrongly, or the father, who was full of grace? It was a lesson I won't forget. The ability to share love and grace rather than judge people comes according to the measure of grace we have received.

And finally, how we deal with grief and understand others who grieve comes from the abundance of grace in our lives. When William Sloan Coffin was the minister at Riverside Church in New York, he lost his 24-year-old son, Alex, in a terrible car accident. He said he received letters, cards, and telephone calls from many friends, all of them well meaning, trying to comfort him but very few of them were helpful.

He said several of them came from fellow preachers, who demonstrated they knew more about the Bible than they knew about the human heart. Coffin says he already knew all the Bible passages. "Blessed are they who mourn for they shall be comforted." "Weeping endures for the night, but joy comes in the morning." He knew all of that, but the depth of his grief made those words unreal to him.[34]

Those who grieve feel like they are in a foreign country where no one speaks their language. Shakespeare said it best (paraphrased), "Everybody knows how to heal grief except those who actually experience it."

Craddock told us of the time when his mother died. He was in line receiving friends when one well intentioned lady said, "I know you are sad, but try to remember where you mother is now and be happy

34 Sermon *Alex's Death*, Riverside Church, New York, January 23, 1983.

for her!" Fred's reply was outstanding, as usual. He said, "When the women went to the tomb of Jesus after his death the angel said to them, 'He is not here. He is risen.' We will have time to celebrate 'she is risen,' but right now, we're dealing with 'she is not here.'"

Those who've been blessed with an abundance of grace are aware of the difficulties at the time of grief and don't attempt to be present with platitudes. They just attempt to be present, and that's grace enough for the occasion.

Gracious folk don't need to have all the answers about anything. They just have all the love in the world to share, and they don't need to get any of the credit for it. They seek only to bless. That's all that really matters, that someday someone can say of you, "He really blessed me." "She really blessed me." No credit is necessary.

There's a wonderful story of a frog and some ducks. Every winter the ducks would fly off to a warmer climate and bid the frog goodbye in his cold mud. He was so envious of the ducks, wishing he could fly away like they did, so he got them all together one day and said, "I've devised a plan for how I can go with you to the warmer climate."

And the ducks said, "We'd take you with us, but you're just too heavy." "I know. I know," said the frog, "But I have a plan. We'll get a long rope and each one of you will take a piece of that rope in your bills and fly parallel to each other. I will clamp my mouth down on the rope too, and you can take me with you!" And they agreed.

It worked for a while. They were flying to a warmer climate, flying real low down over a farm, and the farmer was out in the yard. He looked up and saw that sight and said, "My goodness! What genius thought of that?" And the frog said, "I did." And the farmer had frog legs for dinner.

The result of grace in the human heart is to make a person gracious, and the gracious need no credit for sharing love and grace with others. They're just pleased to do it.

Chapter 11

Never Be Ashamed Of Grace

Paul wrote the Romans, "For I am not ashamed of the gospel; it is the power of God for salvation to everyone who has faith." (Romans 1:16) The gospel of Jesus Christ is about grace, and grace is about love, forgiveness, kindness, and hope. A lot of people in the days of Jesus thought that was not manly enough. After all, they thought the Messiah would be a military hero. To this day, some people think the gospel is weakness. One man said as he went out the door of the church where I was filling in one Sunday, "It's good to have a different voice in the pulpit. I get so tired of hearing our preacher talk about love, love, loooove." Maybe that's why some preachers don't stick with grace. They don't want to be called soft, weak, liberal, or anything like that.

But Paul said, "I'm not ashamed of the gospel. It's the way God has chosen to save the world." When Martin Luther King taught the way to seek civil rights is the way of non-violence, a lot of his followers fell away because they thought it wasn't tough enough. All we have to do is to look at the life of Jesus to realize what a strong man it took to be a man of grace. There was nothing weak about Jesus. Most of the tough guys then and now could not endure what he endured for the sake of you and me.

Leslie Weatherhead was a great pastor in London during WWII. For three years he spent almost every night in the underground stations with the people of London, leading prayers and helping calm anxiety.

He also helped to disarm their hatred of Germans whose bombs and rockets were destroying their city. He spoke often of the need to forgive our enemies and to find forgiveness for our own failures and shortcomings. Week after week, he preached about this in the city temple.

He described God's work of forgiveness in terms of the old sludge boats that once carried off sewage from the city of London. This was before they had modern sewage systems.

He said you could see the little sludge boats lining up at the docks and having the waste pumped into them. Then, one by one they would sail off toward the mouth of the Thames and out into the ocean. Hundreds of miles out, they would dump their burdens into the sea. There, within minutes, the sea would work its magic, churning filth over and over until the water was pure and clean again.

Life in London would have been unthinkable without those sludge boats. The city would have been unbearable. The same would be true for a world like ours if it were not for God's love and forgiveness. They are the sludge boats of the spirit, carrying away the anger, guilt, hostility, and making life livable again. That's what Weatherhead said, and I believe he's right.

Again, and again, we fall on this journey of faith. We never have it mastered. But Jesus said of us in a prayer to God, "They are yours." (John 17:9) That will never change. We are on a journey of progress, and even though we sin, we no longer belong to sin. We belong to God.

Robert Dykstra was a pastoral care teacher at Princeton. He said that when he was a student there he lived near the campus in a beautiful home. It was the home of a woman who had just about everything, and she kept students in her home.

Her dining room contained a beautiful crystal vase of Steuben glass. It was her treasured possession. She filled it with flowers and when the light hit that glass it was pure elegance. While she was away on vacation, another student living in the house emptied some dead flowers from the vase, and while she was doing that, she dinged the vase on the sink and cracked it all the way down from top to bottom.

The student was horrified and began to cry. What would she do? She decided there was nothing she could do but wait for the woman's return to show her what she had done. But later she had an idea. "I'll call the Steuben glass company and see if they can repair it."

When she checked with them, they said they were sorry but that particular piece of glass was out of production. They didn't make it anymore. They could not repair it.

But then they said something that took the young girl's breath away. They said, "If you will bring the broken pieces to our shop in nearby New York, an artist will fashion a replacement at our expense. We will copy and replace it at no charge." Steuben offered to bear the high cost of what had been broken and make it new again.[35] Imagine the relief that girl felt! But the good news of the gospel says that's what God does with you and me every day.

Weak, flawed, sinful, fallen, but God says, "Bring me the broken pieces of your life and I will make it new again at no cost to you. It's on the house. I will pay the high cost." Nothing will ever separate us from the love of God. Two steps forward and one step back, God will be with you throughout your life to pick you up when you fall and to find you when you've become lost. No wonder Paul said, "I'm not ashamed of the gospel."

There is a women's singing group called Sweet Honey in the Rock, who have been around for some time now. They're a Grammy Award winning African-American female acapella group. One of their songs is titled "In My Mama's House There Were No Mirrors." One of the singers has explained how the song was written.

A friend of hers was in a poor neighborhood and had to be raised by her grandmother, and there were no mirrors in her grandmother's house. She didn't own a single mirror, so the girl's friends all asked her, "How did you know what you looked like when you stayed there?"

The girl said, "My Nanna told me. Every morning I would get up, and get dressed, and comb my hair, and then I would go to my Nanna and ask her how I looked. She would say, 'You look beautiful, child. Your skin is smooth and golden brown, kissed by the sun. Your eyes look like stars in the sky. You are absolutely beautiful.'" And the girl said, "There were no mirrors in my Nanna's house, so I saw myself

35 "Princeton Seminary Bulletin", no. 2, vol. XX (1999), 183-188.

through Nanna's eyes."[36]

The grace of God makes it possible for you to see yourself through God's eyes. No matter who you are or what you may have done, you still look beautiful to God, because you are his child. God loves you that much, still believes in your future, and forgives you for the past. That's the description of God's grace. Who could ever be ashamed of that?

You and I live our lives on strong promises. God is saying to us even now, "What Jesus has shown you about me is the truth, I promise you. My mercy is everlasting and I won't change my mind, I promise you. My grace is greater than your sin, I promise you. You may get lost but I'll find you, I promise you. You may lose your grip on me, but I won't lose my grip on you, I promise you."

When I served the West Hills Baptist Church in Knoxville, Tennessee, I used to email my sermons to friends, who requested them each week. I seldom heard back about them. One friend from Charlotte told me her life was blessed every day, and I was encouraged by that. It may be no surprise to know that this woman is one of the most grace-filled people I have ever known. She went through a battle with breast cancer and came away from it an even kinder person. She is a loving supporter of everyone she knows that must walk through that difficult journey. She has spiritual eyes that see the grace that surrounds her. No wonder she found those sermons helpful and had the grace to encourage me.

Another friend from Nashville said this to me, "I'm reading those sermons you emailed me across the years. I hadn't really been reading them, but I have saved them, and now I'm reading one every day. The other day I read one you sent called "The Beloved," and it has had a remarkable effect on me. I had always heard that God loved me, but something about that sermon made me really *know* I am loved. I'd never really felt it before. I'd never fully understood it before, not like now."

When I heard this, I was dumbfounded. I just tried to put God's love into words. I hadn't heard much about it, and he hadn't even read it for years, but he opened his computer and read it and God did something

36 Ysaye M Barnwell, *No Mirrors in My Nana's House* (New York: Harcourt Publishers, 1998).

with it. God's grace is a mystery. You never know when you might be the bearer of that grace. I was unaware of ever making a difference. But when God's spirit interpreted those words in someone's own understanding, that's the thing grace is made of. Later, two others said they were making books out of the sermons, and I thought I was making no difference to anyone.

There is no person or group of persons that can't be used for the purposes of God. Even when you least expect it, and when it surprises you to learn of it, grace does its mysterious work.

Paul Tournier was an imminent Swiss physician. After he wrote his first book, he went back to his favorite professor at his medical school and said, "Sir, I'd like for you to read my book." The professor accepted the book and read it. Sometime later, as they were talking over dinner, Tournier said, "What did you think about the book?" The professor said, "Your book is marvelous. I think all Christians should read it."

Tournier said, "Professor, I am sorry. I've known you for quite some time, but I didn't know you were a Christian. When did you become one?" And the old professor said, "While I was reading your book."[37] No one should think they are unimportant. To be touched by grace is to become an instrument of grace, and you just never know how or when it might happen.

Gardner Taylor was a wonderful African-American preacher, one of America's greatest. When he was a young man, he thought he wanted to be a lawyer. He was accepted to the University of Michigan law school after graduating from Leland College in Louisiana, where he was the chauffeur for the president of the school to help work his way through school.

He was driving the college car on a little country road from Baton Rouge back to Baker, Louisiana, on an errand for the president. A model-T Ford crossed the highway in front of him. There were two white males in the old car, and one of them was killed immediately.

37 Paul Tournier in "Conversion is Possible for All of Us," ProgressiveChristianity.org. https:// progressivechristianity.org/resources/conversion-is-possible-for-all-of-us/.

It was 1937 in Louisiana, and Taylor was an African-American male. There were only two witnesses and they were both white men. Taylor was scared to death. Fortunately, one of them was a Baptist minister and the other a local farmer, and they told the authorities what had happened.

Of all the possible witnesses to the accident in Louisiana, these two men were Christians. They weren't prejudiced, and they weren't mean, and they saved Dr. Taylor from prison or worse.

Shaken by that experience, Gardner Taylor decided not to go to the University of Michigan Law School, where he had been accepted. Instead he went to Oberlin College School of Theology and became one of the best preachers in the nation, serving the 9,000 members at Concord Baptist Church of Christ in Brooklyn, where he became known as an outstanding civil rights preacher. Two men, who were witnesses to an accident, became instruments of God's grace in ways well beyond their wildest imagination.[38]

In the early '80s I was asked to speak at a conference in Erlanger, Kentucky, just outside Cincinnati. It was an interdenominational gathering that met regularly to discuss a variety of theological issues, sponsored by the Kentucky Council of Churches. This particular conference was on baptism.

Our church in Middlesboro had become known for a stand we had taken the year before the conference. I remember the night I spoke to a room full of open-minded deacons about the subject. I told them that I had always had problems with asking people, who had previously been baptized by sprinkling or pouring in another denomination years before, to be baptized again by immersion.

I told them I embraced our mode of baptism, but baptism was meant to be done at the beginning of a Christian walk or upbringing, not years later. One of our finest members had moved to an assisted living facility in Greensboro, North Carolina, and was welcomed into a Presbyterian congregation that was next door to the assisted living place where she

38 Wayne E. Croft Sr., "Past Masters: Gardner C. Taylor", *Poet Laureate of the Pulpit.* https://www.preaching.com/articles/past-masters/past-masters-gardner-c-taylor-poet-laureate-of-the-pulpit/.

was staying. I explained that if they sent us one of their members, we would not accept them without first rebaptizing them, and that was clearly wrong in my opinion. Some things were meant to be done once, and baptism was one of them. I told them as a matter of conscience I could not bring myself to do it again, so help me God.

They agreed that members of other denominations were fellow Christians, so I said, "Why would we not admit someone into our church when God has already accepted them into God's kingdom?" There were two outstanding leaders in that church, who were the chairman and vice chairman of the deacons. One was educated at Oxford and the other at Yale. Thanks to the leadership of Charles Blakeman and Jake Reams a motion was made, seconded, and passed that we would no longer require rebaptisms.

I was so proud of the deacon body. Their motion was passed by the church, and all went well for a while. But the county Baptist association learned of it and voted to disassociate themselves from our church. It was something that made all the newspapers under the headline, Ecumenism Comes to the Mountains of Kentucky. That's when the Committee of Christian Unity of the Kentucky Council of Churches asked me to speak to the group about our experience.

There were all kinds of ministers at Erlanger Retreat Center that day. Presbyterians, Episcopalians, Lutherans, United Methodists, Disciples of Christ, Roman Catholic, and Eastern Orthodox ministers all gathered, just to mention a few. There were black ministers and white ministers, male and female, people in all kinds of liturgical dress from every corner of Christ's church. I talked to them about our oneness in Christ and our church's stand for that belief. They had never heard of such a Baptist church and were deeply moved by our story.

When I finished my talk and sat back down, they all stood up. For what seemed like three minutes they stood there, some with tears streaming down their faces, and applauded. I thanked them, but they kept right on applauding. They were not just applauding me or our church. They were applauding our unity, and they were applauding what the grace of God had done with a Baptist congregation.

I can truthfully say that I've never felt as close to heaven before or since that day. It was one of the most moving experiences of my life, because I knew that the great cloud of witnesses in heaven was applauding with us. The affirmation of fellow Christians from other rooms of faith in the great house of God brought me to tears. It was a glimpse of heaven, to be sure, and it was pure grace poured upon me.

I must have felt like the minister Fred Craddock heard one Sunday. Fred was visiting in another town, where he'd been giving lectures and had found a church in which to worship. The minister was a very large man. His head was misshapen and large, and he wore thick glasses.

As one of the members left the church that day she said to the preacher, "I wish I knew your mother," and the minister replied, "My mother's name is Grace." Fred waited to speak to the man and said, "I heard what that woman said to you, but I was more interested in your answer, your mother's name is Grace."

The minister said, "Yes, when I was born, they didn't want me. They gave me to the state. I was put up for adoption, but nobody would adopt me because of my deformities, so it was foster home after foster home after foster home, and when I was sixteen, I wanted to be with other young people. I noticed a lot of them were going to a church. I was afraid at first, but I thought I would try it, so I went where they were, to this church. And it was there that I met Grace, the grace of God, the quiet, powerful, loving grace of God."[39] What an encouraging story that is! It's the story of a church that hadn't fallen away from grace. Just look at the difference it made.

It reminds us that faith is not simply believing in God. Faith is believing that God is good. Faith is believing in the grace of God shown in Jesus Christ.

John L'Heureux is an American author who wrote a story he called *The Expert On God.* It's the story of a priest whose religion caused him to begin to doubt the love and mercy of God. He struggles with it every

39 Fred Craddock, *Craddock Stories* (St. Louis, Missouri: Chalice Press, 2001), 49-50.

day of his life.

One day, following a church service, the priest was driving home and came upon an accident. He found a young man, dying, trapped in an overturned car. The priest got out and forced the door open, then managed to cradle the dying man in his arms.

Reaching for a vial of holy oil in his pocket, the priest did what he had been trained to do. He anointed the dying man's forehead and said, "I absolve you from all your sins, in the name of the Father, and of the Son, and of the Holy Spirit. Amen." And then there was quietness. No noise. No help coming. No word from heaven. All he can hear is the young man's harsh, half-choked breathing.

The priest didn't know what to do next. He recited some prayers from his prayer book. Then there was nothing but the harsh breathing again. It was quiet. What should he do? What should he say?

The priest, who had been driven to doubt, now asked himself, "What would God do if God were here?" And the question became, "What will God do through me?"

That's when the priest leaned over into the boy's face, which was looking back up at him, and he whispered down to the trusting boy, "Son, I love you. I love you. I love you." And he kept saying that until the boy had stopped breathing.[40]

That's who God is. And that's what grace is. I believe we can trust that and, along with Paul, never be ashamed of it.

That is the reason for this book. There is a scarcity of it in America, and it is the responsibility of the church to restore it. I sincerely hope that this brief reminder and its stories of hope have somehow helped with that.

In over forty years of ministry I have discovered that every man and every woman come to faith in their own way. For John, it was when he came to the empty tomb of Jesus. For Thomas, it was when he could touch the hands of Jesus. For Mary Magdalene, it was when Jesus spoke her name. For the rest of the disciples, it was when Jesus appeared to

40 John L. Heureux, *The Expert on God*, in Comedians (New York: Penguin Books, 1990), 34.

them in the upper room. Everyone is different, but God knows us. God knows how to reach all of us in our own unique way. No one understands quite like God, and no one is as loving and merciful as God.

The moralism that is found in so much of Christianity assumes that the righteous are better and more loved in the sight of God. But Jesus doesn't agree. He doesn't agree with our racism, sexism, or moralism, or any other "isms." In Jesus, we see that God loves sinners as much as the chief priest!

It can be summed up in the story of a man that died and went to heaven. Saint Peter was there to meet him at the pearly gates, and said to him, "Here's how it works. You need 100 points to get into heaven. Tell me the good and wise things you have done, and I will give you a certain number of points for each of them."

"Okay," said the man. "I went to church and supported it all my life." "Great! That'll get you two points!" "Two points? Is that all? Well, I kept the Ten Commandments. That should be worth something." "Wonderful! You're the first person we've ever seen up here who's done that. That'll get you three points!" "Only three? I started a soup kitchen and worked in a shelter for homeless people. How does that sound?"

Saint Peter glared at the man and said, "That sounds absolutely impressive. That's good for another two points." "Well, I went on a mission trip and I supported that ministry for the rest of my life, and I helped build houses with Habitat for Humanity." "Great, that's another two points! You're up to nine whole points now!"

"Nine? All that is worth only nine points? At this rate the only way I'm going to make it is by the grace of God!" "Now you're talking," said Peter. That's worth a hundred points! Come on in."

We've been conditioned in our culture to think that everything is about us, what we do and what we don't do. But that's not the gospel. The gospel is about God.

You may be a wonderful person. Your achievements may be

impressive, and you may have many good attributes. Or, on the other hand, you may be a person who has done some bad things in your life, things you are ashamed of and wish you could take back.

Hear the good news once again. The Christian faith is not about you. It's not about how good or how bad you've been. The Christian faith is about a God who loves you so much that he sent his son to forgive you, and to help you, and to change you. *That… is the gospel.*

Take God's grace with you everywhere you go. There is no more sure way of making a change in your life. And brave journey, my friend.